D0961623

The True Tails of
BAKER AND TAYLOR

The True Tails of
BAKER AND TAYLOR

The Library Cats Who Left Their
Pawprints on a Small Town . . .
and the World

JAN LOUCH
WITH LISA ROGAK

THOMAS DUNNE BOOKS
St. Martin's Press
New York

THOMAS DUNNE BOOKS.
An imprint of St. Martin's Press.

www.thomasdunnebooks.com
www.stmartins.com

Designed by Kathryn Parise

The Baker and Taylor Song
appears courtesy of Leslie Kramm Twigg.

Photograph on page 45 courtesy of Thorntown Public Library, Thorntown, IN.
Photographs on pages 78 courtesy of Freedom Public Library, Freedom, NH;
bar-code photo by Elizabeth Rhymer; circulation desk photo by Joel Rhymer.
Photograph on page 110 courtesy of St. Helena Public Library, St. Helena, CA.
Photograph on page 138 courtesy of New Castle Public Library, New Castle, PA.
Photograph on page 162 courtesy of Lyme Public Library, Lyme, CT.

The Library of Congress Cataloging-in-Publication Data
is available upon request.

ISBN 978-1-250-08107-0 (hardcover)
ISBN 978-1-4668-9297-2 (e-book)

First Edition: May 2016

10   9   8   7   6   5   4   3   2   1

For Yvonne Saddler, Bill Hartman,
and the staff at the Douglas County Public Library—old and new—
without whom this story could not be told

CONTENTS

The True Tails of
BAKER AND TAYLOR

INTRODUCTION

————•◦•————

When I was just eighteen months old, way back in the clutches of the Great Depression, people were desperate. The Lindbergh baby had been kidnapped in 1932, and there had been a slew of copycat kidnappings aimed at families that had the appearance of having more than the majority of people back then, which of course didn't take much. Before the crash of 1929, my family had been comfortable enough, but by 1932 the family fortune had pretty much been wiped out, and both my mother and father were working at the only menial jobs they could find. The sole vestige of affluence that remained came in the form of a Craftsman-style house on Kelton Court in Piedmont, California, which made us a prime target.

One day, my mother set me out in the yard in a playpen while she busied herself inside. Scrapper, our fox terrier, sat alongside as I amused myself with my dolls and alphabet blocks.

A car pulled up in front of the house and a man stepped

out. As he approached the playpen, Scrapper uttered a low growl. When the man stretched out his arms to grab me, Scrapper went into the air and aimed straight for the man's jugular.

He missed, but the would-be kidnapper ran back to the car, Scrapper stayed right on his heels, snarling and baring his teeth. My mother came out of the house just in time to see the getaway car speed off. I was safe and Scrapper was a hero.

When my father died almost seven decades later, we found Scrapper's collar and tags tucked in with his valuables. That feisty little dog had played a life-changing role in our lives, and it was one that we never forgot.

Later on in the decade, the Depression had loosened its grip on the nation only to be replaced by the uncertain future that World War II brought to our lives. I turned to our own pets as well as a variety of animals around the neighborhood for some degree of comfort since I spent much of my time by myself. I also looked to books for entertainment and quickly discovered that they too served as a soothing distraction, with the added bonus of opening a window onto the world for me. I was amazed that I could explore it all from my tiny corner of the universe.

I am not ashamed to admit that I became addicted to books in no time at all. After I plowed through my own family's sizable collection and then the public library a few blocks away—where my almost-daily presence and prodigious reading habits greatly annoyed the matronly, dyspeptic librarian—I moved on to the neighbors' unlocked houses (with permission, mostly), which contained absolute treasure troves of books.

I dove right in, and was happiest whenever my two favorite things in the world, reading and animals, would come together. I sat outside in the yard with my nose in a book and a cat or dog would wander close. I'd reach out to caress the furry head while the act of reading brought me to worlds I dreamed of visiting in person, imaginary or not.

And whenever a book was about an animal—as in the Oz books or *Rikki-Tikki-Tavi* by Rudyard Kipling—well, I don't know how life could have ever gotten any better.

I still don't. I had no way of knowing back then that books and animals would always be intertwined for me in one way or another. So as I became an adult and experienced my fair share of life's disappointments—from the strain of a devastating divorce to learning how to adjust to a new life and find a job that didn't sap my energy or my spirit—animals and books continued to provide a welcome escape from the world, even if just for a little while.

The mere idea of having a job where I could be surrounded by both books and animals, well, even that seemed too far-fetched for some of the fantasy stories I loved to devour as a child. But that's just what happened: I found work as a librarian, and then a couple of cats with funny ears named Baker and Taylor came on board as my feline colleagues and friends.

All of us—patrons and staff alike—quickly fell in love with the Scottish Folds. Then after they became the mascots for the Baker & Taylor book wholesaling company, complete strangers fell in love with them, too. Fans called to say hi, wrote letters and sent mash notes—sometimes from their own cats—and made the pilgrimage to my tiny town in the shadow of the Sierra Nevada Mountains of western Nevada to meet them.

"Where are the cats?" was often the first thing out of someone's mouth as soon as they walked through the door. I'd say, "I saw them heading that way about ten minutes ago," and off they'd go. We were a bit surprised, but not entirely, because after all, we loved the cats.

Renowned cat therapist and author Carole Wilbourn put it best: "A library is a perfect abode for a cat. It makes people feel good, and it makes the cat feel good. People come in and say, 'Cats live here.' What could be better?"

Of course, many people already realize this; it's no wonder that millions of people around the world who first saw Baker and Taylor on a poster fell in love with the cats. They served as the perfect symbols for the connection that many people have with both books and cats. Based on my observations from working in a library for almost two decades, I think that people who are avid readers prefer not to interact a lot with other people because communicating with another human tends to interfere with your reading. However, a substitute that does not speak—like a dog, cat, bird, turtle, or whatever—is perfectly fine; the animal is not going to talk back to you, at least not with words. It's the perfect world: you can spend time with both books and animals simultaneously.

Having a couple of cats who lived at the library for almost fifteen years was not always easy, but as the saying goes, it was never dull, which was the case for both staff and patrons alike, as well as for the thousands of visitors who made a special trek to the library just to meet Baker and Taylor.

Today, many people who clamor for the cat calendars and

stand in line to have their picture taken with the humans dressed in Baker and Taylor costumes at the Baker & Taylor booth at library conventions and trade shows have no idea why a pair of Scottish Folds represent the company; they only know that their convention wouldn't be complete without the latest Baker & Taylor book bag with a picture of the cats on it to bring back home.

They also don't know how the cats helped the people who lived in the town around the library as they learned to adjust to development and rapid growth that wasn't always easy to deal with. Or how they helped a sometimes ragtag group of librarians navigate a world of rapidly changing technology.

Or indeed, how they helped one librarian in particular— me—make peace with a whole slew of tough life changes and come out ahead.

Now that I'm retired, though still reading just as many books as ever, I think it's time to tell the story of Baker and Taylor, a couple of cats with funny ears who lived in a library in Minden, Nevada, and helped people in the community and all over the world feel better about reading . . . and themselves.

ONE

———◄►•◄►———

I t was a simple idea, really.

In the early 1980s, Douglas County, Nevada, was desperate for a new library. The population had tripled in the past decade, and we were rapidly running out of room in the old library. New residents and old-timers jostled for space at the reading tables, elbows touching more often than not.

The bookshelves were so crowded that we had to store the fiction collection in the library director's garage a few blocks away. Whenever a patron wanted to check out a novel or short-story collection, instead of taking the book from the stacks he'd hand over a request with a book title scrawled on it, and once a day a staff member would get in her car, head for the garage, gather up all the books requested, and drive them back to the library for the patrons to pick up.

Even though the library only had two full-time employees and one part-timer, our work area was also pretty cramped. We did everything on a big worktable in the back room, from typing index cards for the card catalog to covering and repairing books. We had one typewriter—a manual—between us. The library director, Yvonne Saddler, sat on one side, me on the other, and we'd rotate the typewriter back and forth, depending upon who needed it most.

On that typewriter, I also pecked out an occasional column for the *Record-Courier,* the local newspaper where I reviewed some of the new books that were on our shelves. The length of the column depended on how much ad space was sold that week. Fewer ads and the editor would lop off the last two books in the column, so I always pushed my favorites to the beginning. The paper had held a contest to name the column and the winning entry was "Read It and Reap." There's nothing I hate more than a bad pun, but it came in first so I had no choice in the matter.

Since I'd started my job as assistant librarian in 1978 at the age of forty-seven, I often had to pinch myself. I'd been addicted to books for as long as I could remember, and I had long dreamed of spending my workdays surrounded by books. Now I was working in a library, as well as helping to plan a new one. We'd received a grant to build a new facility and Yvonne and I started to work with a local architect on the building plans. He knew nothing about libraries and we knew nothing about designing them, but we both started in our respective corners of knowledge and somehow muddled our way through.

We knew what we *didn't* want: our current building. Douglas County's first library was built in 1967, and 4,600 square feet wasn't much space to fit a small collection of books, reading tables, storage, and our workspace.

What we *did* want: hmm . . . where should we start? We

needed a kiosk for new books, a separate room where people could read magazines, this many shelves for fiction, that many for nonfiction, more for biography and reference, and so on. We also had to decide the number of toilet stalls, how to heat the building, and how many chairs and tables we needed for the meeting room. The fact that we actually were going to *have* a meeting room made Yvonne and me feel quite giddy at times.

We were working long days, but compared to the jobs I'd had in the past, I not only loved going to work but also loved that people actually wanted to hear my ideas and opinions. For the first time in my life, I was making decisions that would affect a lot of people and didn't have to pass them through a whole bunch of higher-ups. And for the time being, making do with such cramped quarters was worth it.

❦

After several years of planning, the new library finally opened on July 22, 1982. The months building up to the grand opening were some of the most hectic I've ever experienced in my life. Volunteers and staff alike moved all of the books from the old building to the new library, and helped shelve them according to the Dewey decimal system. We also had to move some of the old furniture, but given that the new space was more than twice the size of the old building, we also had to schedule deliveries of new furniture, bookshelves, and equipment, and then set them up.

Not only did we have to move and organize books, furniture, and office equipment, but we also had to arrange books on the shelves and get accustomed to working in a completely new environment. In fact, in order to cut down on the number of books we had to move, we told patrons they could check out as many books as they liked and to keep them until we moved into the new building, and we wouldn't charge them any overdue fines.

The gap between the old library closing and the new one opening was about three weeks, and so when we reopened we were mobbed, because patrons were so eager to check out books again. Both the move and getting settled took a lot out of people, but by the same token it brought us closer together because we all had a common goal: to make our new library the best it could be.

We were totally exhausted, but we were all proud of what we had accomplished. We had a brand-new library and I could look around at something that I'd had a hand in creating.

⸻◈⸻

The new library had been open for a few weeks when Yvonne and I took a break and headed into the reading room, which looked out onto a patio.

Out of the corner of my eye, I saw a patch of grass rustle. The winds coming down off the Sierra Nevada Mountains can be so relentless and fierce that the trees lining U.S. 395—the main highway through town—actually grow at an angle, pointing away from the mountain range. But it wasn't windy that day.

We saw a small gray blur fly past on the patio. A mouse. Then another.

The library had been built on an alfalfa field, and where there's alfalfa, there are mice. Lots of them.

My eyes shifted to Yvonne. "Looks like those mice mean business." I paused. "Are you thinking what I'm thinking?"

"I'm way ahead of you," she replied. "We *do* have an obligation to protect the taxpayers' investment." After all, books are bound with glue, which is as irresistible to rodents as catnip is to cats. In fact, in the old library, I once picked up a sponge with two long-dead desiccated mouse carcasses stuck to it. Not one to shriek, I calmly placed it back in the soap dish and dealt with it later.

A bigger library meant more books and glue, and therefore more mice.

"A cat in the library," I said.

"Maybe two," Yvonne volleyed back just as another mouse skittered by.

I nodded. "One cat would get lonely at night and when the library's closed."

"Two cats could keep each other company," said Yvonne.

"Two are better," I said. "After all, there will be lots of new books."

"And we have to protect them."

We stared at the moving grass—upon closer inspection, we discovered that it was actually a kind of mouse highway—and proceeded to hatch the idea that would change both our lives.

Even though I only had two cats at home and Yvonne had one, the world would probably call us crazy cat ladies. Every year when the Silver State Cat Show was held in Reno, we'd dutifully make the trip and spend a good part of each day oohing and aahing at the different breeds of cats. We were particularly fond of the British shorthairs, a bulky breed with a squarish head and a mouse-gray fur so deep and thick that you could easily bury your fingers in their coats up to the second knuckle.

We liked the breed because we were both fervent Anglophiles, at least when it came to reading material. More than a handful of patrons and librarians from elsewhere had commented on the library's expansive collection of books by British authors. I had lived in the U.K. during the early years of my marriage, and Yvonne had frequently traveled there, so we were well aware that the vast majority of libraries throughout England—both public and even some academic—had a cat or two on the payroll to keep the vermin away, and so did many bookstores.

There were other similarities: we both had gray hair and were close in age—Yvonne was four years older—though I was a bit taller, but there were also significant differences. While I had been working at my dream job for only a few years, Yvonne was a career librarian, and because she served as the face of the library, she was always more put together than I was. People don't realize that working in a library can be a pretty dirty job, between kneeling on the floor to reshelve books, opening scuffed cartons of new books that had been shipped thousands of miles, and leafing through old books covered with a thick layer of dust. So I tended to wear older, occasionally ratty clothes to work while Yvonne was far more stylish and much more professionally dressed so she'd be taken seriously by county commissioners and government officials.

When we attended the cat show in 1982, we took a particular liking to a stocky British shorthair named Tank. He scooched up against the side of his cage and purred like a chain saw while we scratched behind his ears and cooed at him.

As we made our way through the show, we spotted a Scottish Fold, a breed that was new to us. Since we were both part Scottish—Yvonne was Scottish-French-English while I'm Scottish-Italian-English—we were intrigued.

A close relative to the British shorthair, the Scottish Fold had fur that was equally dense, though his eyes were rounder and bigger. And his ears were creased, folded close to his head. The cat looked somewhat like an owl, wise and curious about everything around him. He seemed friendly yet slightly reserved.

We read the information card hanging on the cage, and found out the first Scottish Fold—named Susie—was born near Dundee, Scotland, in 1961. The ear folds are the result of a genetic abnormality that affects not only the ears but also the cartilage all throughout the body. All Scottish Folds are born with straight ears, which "fold" by the time they're a month old; if they don't fold by that time, they won't fold at all. If they do fold, they can be single—which creases halfway—or a double or triple fold, which are much closer to the head. In the case of a triple fold, the ears almost touch the skull.

As we did with Tank, we scratched and cooed and daydreamed of bringing this owlish cat home with us, but we knew that the current feline residents at our respective homes wouldn't stand for another addition. But maybe there'd be a place at the library?

Purebreds were a bit of an anomaly for Douglas County and the Carson Valley—the region south of Reno and east of Lake Tahoe—in the early 1980s, where the vast majority of cats lived in the barns of the many cattle ranches and dairy farms that dotted the area. Though they interacted with humans, most of the cats were borderline feral; they'd approach you with great hesitation if you offered a can of tuna or handful of kibble, but for the most part they kept their distance.

I lived on my parents' ranch with my children in the tiny town of Genoa—the first settled town in Nevada and one town over from Minden—and even though we had barn cats, we also kept a couple of well-loved house cats named Big and Little who lived in the lap of luxury inside.

The local hardware store had a resident orange tabby cat who spent his days sleeping in a coiled-up rubber hose in the front display window, which I thought set a good precedent for us getting a cat for the library. He was there for years and nobody had any problem with him. There'd also been cats in other businesses in town, including the florist shop.

Once we made the decision to add a couple of feline employees to our staff, we figured that the library board didn't have to know about it. After all, we'd be the ones who would be taking care of the cats and covering all of their expenses.

But first we had to overcome one small obstacle: money. As librarians working in a small rural county, we weren't exactly rolling in it. And we also couldn't ask taxpayers to cover the cost.

So while Yvonne and I saved our pennies, we started to think about names that would be appropriate for a pair of felines who lived in a library. We briefly considered Dewey and Decimal but we already knew of several library cats with those names. Another short-lived idea was Volume I and Volume II, but thankfully neither of us took that one seriously.

"How about Page?" Yvonne offered.

I shook my head. "The second cat would have to be named

Turn, or Cover. For that matter, I think we can forget about Hardcover and Paperback."

We tossed a few other ideas back and forth but nothing clicked. I pondered some more as I began to unpack the boxes of new books that had arrived that morning. As I opened the first box, that's when it hit me.

Baker & Taylor—the name of the library wholesaler that shipped the vast majority of books to the library—was stamped all over the box. I had emptied countless Baker & Taylor boxes in my day before cataloging and shelving new books. More important, the names seemed to fit a breed of cat with folded ears who looked like owls.

I tested the names out in my head. "Baker, dinnertime! Taylor, I bought you a new catnip mouse!"

I passed it by Yvonne, and she agreed.

Baker and Taylor it would be.

TWO

─◆─◆─◆─

Ｗe contacted a Scottish Fold breeder from the cat show, who told us she had a gray and white male with a slightly abnormal spine, so he couldn't compete in any cat shows, but that he'd make a perfectly capable library cat. She added that he was pretty calm but also loved people.

He sounded like a good fit. Since we first made our decision, Yvonne and I had drawn up a list of characteristics for our ideal library cat: in addition to having a superb talent at mousing, he had to be mellow in the face of squealing, sticky-fingered toddlers at story time, and gregarious enough to deal with teenagers and adults who loved cats so much they might pursue him around the library in order to get in a few pats and ear scratches.

The breeder told us she'd let us have him at a discount: ninety bucks. From our years going to the cat show, we knew that exotic breeds were more expensive, and since Scottish Folds were still relatively rare in the U.S., most cats cost several hundred dollars or more, which was a lot of money at the time for a couple of county government employees. He would come already neutered, which would save us even more money.

The breeder set the delivery date for March 10, 1983, and we got busy. We bought toys, cat food, bowls for food and water, and a litter box, which we put in the storage closet to provide adequate privacy. I was glad we had decided, when we were planning the new library, to put the storage closet in the staff room instead of in the meeting room, which wouldn't always be open.

The day finally came when he was due to arrive.

"How'd you sleep last night?" Yvonne asked.

I pointed at the dark circles under my eyes.

We couldn't focus on stamping books, and while doing research for a patron, I ended up reading the same sentence for fifteen minutes before I finally gave up.

Finally, a little before noon, a woman walked through the door with a cat carrier.

"He's here!"

We all rushed toward the front of the library. The breeder set the carrier on the floor, unlatched the door, and we all peered inside. The cat blinked and took a couple of steps forward so he was half in and half out of the carrier. He sniffed the air, took another few steps, and suddenly a plethora of arms all reached toward him.

He stood calmly as we all started to pet him at once. We showed him the location of his food and water bowls and litter box, and then tried to let him be. That plan lasted for all of two seconds as a small crowd of librarians and patrons proceeded to follow him around for the rest of the day. I don't have to tell you that very little work got done.

While the others were fawning all over him, I looked at his registration papers.

BIRTHDATE: OCTOBER 6, 1981.
NAME: McLEAN'S CLINT EASTWOOD.

I don't think so. This cat was far from having a lean and hungry look. In fact, he was the epitome of roundness: round head and body, round eyes, and with the same ultraplush fur that Tank had.

I thought he looked more like a Baker than a Taylor. He had white and gray markings with a thin white stripe up the middle of his face, and with his big white belly he looked a little like the Pillsbury Doughboy, so we settled on Baker because he looked like a baker, sort of doughy. Besides, Yvonne and I thought the name Taylor sounded like it would belong to a more refined cat.

At the end of the first day, I locked the doors, turned off the lights, and brought Baker into the staff room. I patted his bed and he jumped onto it. He looked at me quizzically, as if to say *Okay, now what?*

"I'll be back in the morning," I told him, petting his head. I thought he looked a bit lonely, but maybe I was projecting because I knew *I'd* miss him. I was even more determined to scrimp and save for Taylor, especially after I saw how both patrons and staff members lit up at the sight of just one cat. In barely a few hours, Baker had absolutely changed the library for the better.

And, I also had to admit, I was being a bit selfish. Books and cats were two of my favorite things in the world and now I was surrounded by both all day long. How could it get any better?

———✦———

When a cat arrives in a new place, he does one of two things: he either picks a spot where you'll never find him and hides out for at least a few days, or else he'll be curious and explore everything in sight from the get-go. Baker clearly fell into the second category. He spent his first few days at the library wandering and sniffing and touring up and down the aisles so he could scrutinize every square inch of the place. He reminded me of the building inspectors who came to check out the new library after each stage of construction was completed; nothing escaped their notice.

By the end of the first week, Baker had made himself right at home. It was not uncommon to see him jumping onto the tops of the bookshelves, sleeping on somebody's purse, or pushing someone's books out of the way so he could get more comfortable, trying to get a few extra head scratches in along the way. He accepted lots of petting, and didn't recoil from endless squeals of "Oooh, a cat!" from adults and children alike. And if a patron was standing in the New Books section when he happened to stroll by, he'd start playing with their shoelaces.

One day, not long after Baker had settled in, I watched as Constance Alexander, one of our new librarians, petted and fussed and cooed to him. We were at the circulation desk, and already Baker had picked a couple of favorite spots: directly under the skylight, especially if the sun was out, or in a box of voter registration forms because, well, it was a box.

It wasn't long before we could tell time by where Baker happened to be. We'd tell people, "If you're looking for Baker, look for the sun." Nine times out of ten that's where he'd be. It was obvious he liked a toasty atmosphere.

Like us, Constance had cats at home—most of her cats were mixed breeds and rescued tabbies—so she knew how to deal with the feline temperament. After a few minutes I asked her, "So what do you think?"

Her fingers were buried in his fur and I don't think I'd ever seen her grin that big. "He's definitely a teenager," she said. "He looks like part of four different cats put together."

Indeed, at eighteen months old, Baker's head was very large but his body was long, and his legs were still a bit stubby. "He'll grow into a beautiful cat," she said.

⟡

Even though we had hired Baker to keep the mice out and I was all ready to order business cards for him with the title of Mouse Catcher, after he moved in, we never saw another mouse. Rodents can smell cats and once they know there's a cat in the house they tend to stay far away, even if there's food around.

Instead, it became clear that his main job was turning out to be Official Greeter. Baker quickly zeroed in on the circulation desk as his primary space. There, he—like us—could both welcome people as they came in the door and keep an eye on things. He helped supervise us at the circ desk in between sprawling across the counter to present his belly to be rubbed by any and all comers.

I sometimes thought that Baker had an unwritten deal with patrons: three scratches behind the ear and thirty seconds of belly rubbing were required for each book you check out today. Of course, most patrons happily complied, and then some.

Word of our new resident spread quickly around town, and it didn't take long before more people came to visit the library. As soon as they walked through the sliding glass doors, we'd hear, "Where's the cat?" Patrons were clearly tickled by the novelty of checking out a few books while Baker wove figure eights around their ankles or assisted with duties at the circulation desk by shedding a few stray hairs into the pocket for the date-due card.

One day, a young girl, maybe around three, came over. "Kitty!" she squealed, and thrust a sticky hand into Baker's coat.

Baker's ears twitched slightly but he stayed put.

I breathed a sigh of relief. It was going to work after all. We had hired the perfect cat for the job. Now all we needed to do was find our Taylor. I still felt bad about leaving Baker alone by himself at night, and tuned the radio to a local classical station before I left at the end of the day. In the morning he was so eager for company he tripped me more often than not when I walked in the door, and then followed close on my heels as I went about the process of opening the library for the day and feeding him, scooping the litter box, and changing the water in his bowl.

But acquiring Baker had just about cleaned both Yvonne and me out financially. Even if we ate nothing but pasta for the next few months, it would be a struggle to scrape together the money for another cat.

<hr/>

A few days after Baker arrived at the library, Joyce Hollister, a reporter from the *Record-Courier,* the local newspaper, showed up at the library to write an article about our new employee. After the story and a couple of photographs were splashed across the front page, even more people flocked to the library, including some whom I'd never seen walk through the doors, both newcomers to the region and old-time ranching families.

"You have a cat in the library?" they'd ask, with either a note of anticipation or trepidation coloring their voices.

I nodded. "Soon we'll have two."

The day the story appeared, it was my turn to open the boxes of new books. We rotated jobs each day, from covering books and entering the data for each book into the catalog, to manning the desk. I never got tired of seeing and holding a new book in my hands. I even held them up to my nose to smell. Each one represented new adventures and knowledge, something I didn't know before. Too bad my job left little time for reading; I managed what I could at night in between taking care of my own cats, but there was never enough time to read.

The great irony of working in a library.

As I opened another carton of books with Baker & Taylor splashed all over the box, it occurred to me that the company might like to hear about their feline namesake as well as our plans to complete the pair.

I dropped some newly covered books on Yvonne's desk all ready to be shelved. "Maybe you should tell Bill Hartman about Baker," I told her. "He'd get a kick out of it."

Bill Hartman was the sales and marketing director for the western division of Baker & Taylor, and served as our primary contact with the company. He'd pop into the library every couple of months or so to gab about new books and poke around the library.

"I'm way ahead of you," said Yvonne, who explained that she'd already sent him a copy of the newspaper story with a note telling him that we were busily saving up our spare change so we could add Taylor to the staff.

We heard from Bill a couple of days later, and he said he was honored that we'd decided to name our cats after the company. He offered to contact a few of the trade magazines like *Publishers Weekly* and *Library Journal* about doing stories on the cats after Taylor arrived. Yvonne and I were thrilled at the prospect of receiving national publicity for our tiny small-town library.

But we knew that would be months in the future. In the meantime, we busied ourselves with making our newest staff member feel at home, as well as deal with a growing library.

You see, Baker wasn't the only reason why library usage was up. The entire Carson Valley was undergoing a radical growth spurt against the backdrop of a severe recession. Many people—especially retirees—were getting fed up with the high taxes and housing costs in California and were moving to Nevada, which had no income tax. They could buy a much bigger house here for a fraction of what they sold their California house for, which meant they had a good chunk of change left over to live on. Plus, you had space to breathe in Nevada; the valley spread out for miles around and we were a short drive from Lake Tahoe.

What's more, it was downright beautiful. After all, that's why my parents had moved here in the 1960s. My father wanted to live in the mountains and raise some animals, and you couldn't really do that in most parts of the Bay Area where they had lived previously.

Naturally, more new residents meant more library patrons. So though we would have liked to have Taylor sooner, we resigned ourselves to the fact that we shouldn't hold our breath. Besides, we had plenty of work on our plates.

◆◆◆

About a month after Baker arrived, he was lying on a pile of papers on my desk taking his third nap of the day. That cat did love to sleep. He also needed an occasional break from his adoring public, and he'd scoot into the staff room where he'd be sure to get a treat or two from the stash we kept in the closet. I was catching up on my correspondence when the phone rang. Bill Hartman was on the other end.

I wanted to ask him about a few new books I'd read about in *Library Journal*. "Hold on a minute." I dug through my desk for the issue and found it under a catnip mouse. "Ready?"

"That can wait," he said. "I have some good news for you. How would you like to have Taylor sooner rather than later?"

"Unless we win the lottery, that's not going to happen," I told him.

He laughed. "How about if we buy Taylor for you?"

I almost dropped the phone. Constance mouthed *What?* in my direction.

"Why?" I asked him.

He told me that after Yvonne told him about Baker, he started thinking. "I've been to hundreds of libraries all over the country through the years, and almost every one of them had one thing in common: *cats.* Not real ones like yours, but pictures, posters, and figurines. People who work in libraries love cats. So maybe if we put together a poster of two cats that were actually named Baker and Taylor and also lived in a library, librarians would love it."

He'd get no argument from me. We'd all felt the change at the library in just a few weeks. "So would patrons," I said, a bit cautiously, not wanting to jinx anything. "Go on."

"We've been looking for some type of promotion to do within libraries and at conventions," Bill continued. "The whole idea is to get people into our booth at conferences, and I think the cats will help. At least they have to be better than what we currently use."

I had to agree. The freebies Yvonne had brought back from the last American Library Association convention consisted of a horseshoe-shaped key chain and a nondescript black paperweight with BAKER & TAYLOR CO. etched on it, which she promptly tucked away in her desk, unused and gathering dust ever since.

"You probably know that we're not the most warm and fuzzy company out there," he said, and we both laughed. While Baker & Taylor wasn't a company on the scale of a General Electric, when compared to other library wholesalers and distributors it was still very big for the industry. Using a couple of cats to market the company to librarians would make Baker & Taylor seem more approachable and personable instead of just another big corporate entity. And though I loved the books that came out of their boxes, Bill was right: the company was pretty stodgy.

"So we'll buy Taylor for the library if you let us take a few pictures and make a poster out of it," he said. "We'll both come out ahead."

The deal sounded almost too good to be true, but if it meant we could get our Taylor faster, I was all for it.

"So what do you think?"

I tried to quash my excitement, but I knew I wasn't doing a very good job. "I'll have to pass it by Yvonne first," I told him, though I couldn't imagine she'd refuse the offer.

I hung up the phone and ran into her office.

"What's the matter?" she asked.

As I described Bill's offer to her, she started smiling. Five minutes later, I was back on the phone giving him the names and numbers of several Scottish Fold breeders.

I couldn't believe my luck. On a handshake deal, we'd soon have two cats in the library and Baker would have a companion. I thought that having a photographer take a few rolls of film was a fair deal in exchange. Plus, we'd get some posters of the cats as a neat souvenir.

———— ◦•◦ ————

We were so happy to be getting another cat in the library that we really didn't care what he or she looked like in terms of color and markings, only that it was a Scottish Fold. So when Bill said he had found a brown and white tabby at a cattery in Washington State that was ready to go, we quickly agreed. Part of me was afraid he'd change his mind, since I felt that we were so clearly getting the better end of the deal.

The new cat had already made a splash on the cat-show circuit, chalking up four wins in one show. He cost $250, and shipping was an extra $76. It would have taken us some time to save up that kind of money.

On May 17, 1983, I picked Taylor up at the Reno airport. I talked to him and rested my hand against the door of the cage. He sniffed it a couple of times and mostly stared at me for the entire ride.

He was born on July 7, 1982, and just like Baker, arrived with a registered name that was pretty ridiculous: Kareem Abdul-Jabbar, who was a seven-foot-two-inch African-American basketball player.

When we got back to the library, I set the carrier down in the workroom, gathered everyone around, and brought Baker over so he could witness the momentous event as well. I opened the door of the carrier, and Taylor tentatively poked his head out, but then he immediately ran under my desk. I shooed everyone away except Baker, and got down on my hands and knees to comfort the cat, who had wedged himself back behind my desk and the wall.

I've had cats do this before when I first brought them home. They're so freaked out by the rigors and stress of the trip, and when they set foot in a new place with a crowd of new faces surrounding them, all wanting a touch and a hug, well, I'd freak out, too.

Taylor stayed under the desk for three days, at least during the hours when humans were around. I slid bowls of food and water under the desk, and the following morning I had to refill them, though of course, it could have been Baker helping himself, since he had already proven himself to be a bit of a chowhound, cleaning his bowl free of every stray bit of kibble and then longingly staring at us while we ate our lunches at our desks.

But Baker was just as curious about the new arrival as we were, and a couple of times over those first few days I saw him duck under my desk. Once I peeked and saw them rubbing noses and I sensed he was welcoming Taylor and reassuring him that the library wasn't such a bad place to be. I didn't hear any hissing or yowling, so at least they were getting along with each other.

On the fourth day, Taylor finally emerged from his hiding place and tentatively began to explore the library. Baker helped provide moral support here and there, accompanying Taylor as he took his first hesitant steps toward the stacks. Soon Taylor wandered off on his own, sniffing at books on the shelves and testing the carpet with his claws, but he always returned to the workroom after a few minutes.

I was at my desk working away to make up for the time I had spent driving up to Reno to pick him up. Since we had moved to the new library, I now had an IBM Selectric to call my own and I still reveled in it, so I was absorbed in my typing when I felt a pair of eyes boring into the side of my face. Taylor was sitting at my feet, looking intently at me as though I was the most interesting person in the world.

I reached down to pet him, but he continued to stare at me. "What do you want?" I asked him, and stared back. But I was the first to blink.

His gaze remained unbroken. Did he even have eyelids? Later on, we would joke that Taylor could win a staring contest with a fish.

Maybe he was hungry. As soon as I stood up, he immediately jumped onto my chair and up onto my desk. He then proceeded to rustle a stack of papers together for a makeshift bed, and then performed the universal cat dance—a few twirls clockwise, then counterclockwise, front paws pumping slightly up and down on top of the papers as he tried to find the best spot, and finally plopping himself down with a satisfied sigh— that signified it was time for a nap.

"Oh, Taylor, I need those papers," I said, then stopped. I could always get them later and work on something else in the meantime. After all, just as the cats had to adjust to a new life in the library, so did we. And if it made our new arrival feel better by perching on top of a stack of interlibrary-loan requests, then so be it.

So far, no one in the library—patron or staffer—seemed to have an issue with the cats. I knew that would change; after all, not everyone loved cats. But for the time being Baker and Taylor had caused a definite positive shift in the library. People were happier, the mood was lighter, and even patrons and staff who usually began their day somewhat grumpy were acting differently.

And I included myself in that last category.

◆◆◆

It soon became clear that while the two cats shared a breed and lineage—Taylor was actually Baker's nephew—they were miles apart in terms of temperament. While Baker followed the sun in the main room and camped out on the front desk and by the door so he could suck up to patrons, Taylor quickly demonstrated that he wasn't terribly interested in greeting the public; small doses would do it for him.

Instead, he spent most of the day in the workroom, camped out on whichever stack of papers I happened to need at that particular moment.

In fact, in his short time at the library, Taylor hadn't zeroed in on anyone else, either patron or staff. Just me. The thought had occurred to me that since I was the one who had picked him up at the airport, he may have naturally imprinted on me as *the one,* much like a duckling or chick instantly gloms on to the first living, breathing creature it sees after fighting its way out of its shell.

Yvonne had welcomed the cats and spent some time with them, but as head of the library she worked in a separate office and often had to travel out of town on library business, so she wasn't always around. And when she was, her door was often closed. Since my desk was in the workroom along with the cat food, toys, and litter box, it was understandable that the pattern was set early on for me to assume responsibility for making sure that the cats had everything they needed, and also to step in to protect them in case a patron got a little too rambunctious.

The next time Taylor left my desk to make his all-too-brief rounds out in the library, I decided to make a bed for him that would be much more comfortable than my papers. I pulled out an old afghan from the lost and found box we kept under the circulation desk and shaped it into a nest at the corner of my desk. When Taylor sauntered back in, he promptly hopped right onto the stack of interlibrary-loan requests and began his preparations for a long afternoon nap.

Constance watched me. She was a cat lover, so she knew Taylor was playing me.

I patted the afghan. Taylor lifted his head, heaved his body up, and arranged himself on top of the afghan nest.

"I'm impressed," said Constance. "Most cats would totally ignore you."

"Taylor isn't like most cats," I said, and resumed typing.

That much was already clear.

The next morning, I walked into the workroom and there on the afghan was Taylor, sitting upright, rear legs splayed out in front, front paws resting on his haunches.

He looked like a yogi who'd been interrupted during his meditation session.

While Taylor stared at me, I started laughing and couldn't stop. A couple of the other staff members stuck their heads in the door to see what the commotion was all about. They started to laugh, too.

"I've never seen a cat do that before," said one.

"Is he comfortable?" asked another.

"Did he *break* something?"

Taylor's ears twitched slightly but he stayed put, acknowledging each of us one at a time with a subtle nod as if he was indeed a benevolent Buddha blessing each of us.

"He looks like he's meditating," said Constance. "How did you get him to do that?"

I peered over the tops of my glasses. "I didn't," I said. "You can't make a cat do something he absolutely doesn't want to do unless there's a darn good reason for it."

The breeder had explained to me that the same genetic trait that made Scottish Folds' ears fold down also gave some of the cats a certain ligamentous laxity in their legs and tails. Most Scottish Folds were built so they occasionally sat that way. Something with the genetics responsible for the ears also affects the hips and spine, and made sitting upright most comfortable for him.

So despite our laughter and finger-pointing, Taylor stayed put. He'd continue to sit and I'd keep on laughing. Or he'd stare off into space while pondering the mysteries of the world as well as librarians who couldn't control themselves. A tiny sigh and a huff, then he'd return to his Buddha state.

"Maybe we should have named him Buddha," I said to Yvonne one day after we had caught our breaths after another giggling fit. But Baker & Taylor—the company—probably wouldn't have liked that. Maybe they'd make us give him back . . . or pay for him, which I know we couldn't do.

A couple of days later, I saw Baker assume a variation on the posture, but he was chunkier and it wasn't as comfortable for him. When he did manage to arrange himself upright, he instead leaned over to one side while he propped himself up with one paw, trying his best to look casual.

But the Buddha position was Taylor's default mode. Whenever he ventured out into the main room, he liked to back himself up to the ends of the bookcases and sit there observing the people coming and going. It made him seem like he was a yogi on some faraway mountaintop who had devotees coming from miles around just to see him.

In addition to sitting like a Buddha, Taylor was also a champion snorer. If he was asleep under my desk and a visitor happened to be standing nearby, she usually asked, "What's wrong with your computer?"

Baker and Taylor made us crack up constantly. Even though I saw Taylor in his Buddha pose and Baker in his here's-my-belly-now-rub-it mode every day, I still laughed. We all found it hard not to giggle throughout the day at their antics. And that, in itself, is what set it apart from every other place I had ever worked in my life.

THREE

After only a couple of weeks, it felt like Baker and Taylor had been at the library for years.

They quickly settled into their routines, and so did we, both patrons and staff. We shut them in the workroom at night so they didn't roam all over the library. I've always thought that cats can get a little nervous when they're thrown into a great big empty space with nobody around. And after all, we "hired" them to protect the library, not to destroy it.

Yvonne and I treated Baker and Taylor the same way we treated our own cats at home. In that way, Baker and Taylor's lives weren't radically different from any other house cat. Their home just happened to be a library, and just like any other domestic feline, they absolutely ruled the roost.

What was different, however, was the number and variety of people who interacted with the cats over the course of the day. And so they had a little bit more variety than a typical house cat.

From the moment I arrived at the library in the morning to find the cats waiting at the door eager for me to open a can of cat food to the time in the evening after the library closed when I made sure they had food and water and were secure in the workroom, Baker and Taylor spent their days like most other pampered indoor cats: they'd eat, sleep, use the litter box, have a brief morning wrestling session, and settle down for the first of several naps over the course of the day, all interspersed with occasional head scratches and play time.

When lunchtime rolled around, most of the staff members, myself included, brought our lunches and ate at our desks. The cats were usually interested in checking out that day's menu, but one food in particular would transform Baker from a leisurely cat to an insatiable tiger.

If somebody brought cantaloupe for lunch, Baker would show up in a nanosecond. Even if he was on the other side of the library, once he got a whiff he'd come barreling into the workroom, jump up onto the appropriate desk, and try like mad to steal the cantaloupe. And if the person with said cantaloupe refused, Baker would start dancing with his front feet, as if he was saying *Hurry up, hurry up. I want that more than you do, so you should just give it to me.*

Who knew a cat would love cantaloupe? But he'd eat the whole thing, rind and all. Baker wasn't a very vocal cat, but whenever cantaloupe appeared on the scene, he would emit a very strong, high-pitched mew. Then once he got the fruit between his jaws, he'd carry the cantaloupe around in his mouth and growl at anyone who tried to take it away from him.

Taylor didn't care about cantaloupe; instead, he was an absolute fool for yogurt, but he only liked lemon or vanilla flavors. More than once he got his head stuck in a yogurt container someone had thrown away and would sometimes wander around the library with it still on his head as he licked it clean. Eventually he'd finish but sometimes he couldn't get his head out of the yogurt carton, so we had to come to his rescue.

We were learning that such unusual tasks were all in a day's work.

One day I was out at the circulation desk watching the cats in between stamping date-due cards. Baker was sprawled by the front door lying on his back. Even though he was still a young cat and not what you would think of as plump, his belly was sizable, and whenever a patron came through the door, he'd take a breath as if to present his girth to them, saying *Here it is, the great white belly. Rub it.* That was how he communicated.

Baker was more of a social, happy-go-lucky cat than Taylor. He loved to hang out at the circ desk to make sure books were stamped correctly, that is, when he wasn't fast asleep on the mat that we kept next to the stamp pads and voter registration forms. While Baker focused on making patrons happy, Taylor was more attuned to the staff and was more sensitive to people's moods than Baker was. Whenever Taylor ventured away from the workroom, he liked to sit in his Buddha position with his back up against the copy machine while he fastidiously washed himself, going over the same patch of fur on his paw so many times that I occasionally worried that he'd rub the spot raw and render it furless.

As I chuckled at the differences between them, the old sitcom *The Odd Couple* popped into my head. Of course! Baker was

Oscar Madison—the good-natured, hedonistic slob—while Taylor was Felix Unger, the neurotic neat freak, an old maid of a cat, prim and proper in every way. Plus, while Baker could be oblivious to anything that lay in his path—come hell or high water, he would take his sunbath—Taylor was especially observant, always attuned to any and all activity around the library even if his eyes were closed.

Baker wasn't necessarily an unhygienic cat, but he clearly didn't keep up with Taylor's standards of cleanliness. If Baker was the least bit messy, Taylor couldn't stand it and would start grooming him. And while Baker was a food-oriented cat—even aside from cantaloupe—Taylor was more interested in staying well hydrated. But befitting a Felix Unger type, he pretty much ignored his water bowl which, after all, sat on the floor and who knows what's been in it. Instead he preferred to drink out of the mugs that most of us kept on our desks, which contained water most of the time, but sometimes he wasn't particular and he'd go for coffee or tea in a pinch.

One morning, I was scooping out the litter box when I heard my name.

"Jan?"

"Yes?"

"Your cat is drinking out of my mug again."

Hmph. It's always *our* cat when showing them off to patrons, but *your* cat when they misbehave.

I put down the scoop and headed for the culprit.

"I'll take care of it. Bad boy, Taylor," I said, but my words were devoid of malice. I couldn't help it. How could I get mad at this cat? I rooted around in the storage closet and found a chipped mug with HAPPY BIRTHDAY written on it. I waved it around to the assembled crowd. "Does this belong to anybody?"

No one claimed it, so I filled it with water and set it by Taylor's afghan. "This is yours, so you don't have to touch anyone else's," I told him, and resumed my litter box duties. He sniffed it, took a few sips, and never bothered anyone else's again unless his ran dry.

⸻

By the fall, circulation at the library had increased seventeen percent over the previous year.

It was pretty amusing when some patrons who hadn't been in for a while said, "There's a cat in the library!" And then, a few seconds later we'd hear, "Oh my God, there's another one!" But just like us, they quickly became accustomed to the sight of two cats with funny ears wandering around the stacks, supervising staff at the circulation desk, or just watching the world go by.

I fully realized that part of the reason for the growth was the cats, and another the increase in population of the county, but it was also due to the way the new library was laid out. The old library had had only a few chairs where people could spread out, relax, and read a newspaper or magazine, while the new library had big airy rooms with lots of windows that received the bulk of the morning sun. The reading room was also set away from the rest of the library so it was a lot quieter. As a result, people tended to stick around longer than they did at the old library, regardless of whether one of the cats was supervising their reading sessions. It was kind of amusing to see a couple of men in their fifties, sometimes wearing business suits, sitting in the reading room perusing the *Wall Street Journal*, while Baker sat on a chair in between them.

But I quickly realized that some of the new patrons coming in had never set foot in a public library in their lives. Since Douglas County had only gotten its first library in 1967, there were a lot of people who had lived here all their lives and never had a library except when they were in school. And a lot of times, the school library didn't have much more than first-grade-level reading primers and old textbooks.

So once the cats arrived, these old-time ranchers and fourth- and fifth-generation residents with feral barn cats couldn't get over the idea of keeping a cat in a house, let alone a library. So they came to see for themselves. And for the first time in their lives, they learned how to use the library.

After they signed up for their first-ever library card, they stood at the New Books section scanning the display while Baker polished their ankles in a figure eight. They picked up a book and took it home to read. And when they came back to return it and perhaps take out another, the cats were there to greet them like old friends.

In a way, the cats were like a gallon of milk at a convenience store, loss leaders: people came for the cats and stayed for the books. And so the cycle began, and the number of user visits and circulation increased.

In the early afternoon, there was usually a bit of a lull at the library; the patrons who came in the morning and others who returned a few books on their lunch hour were gone. The next rush consisted of the high school kids who would come in to do their homework. We got a lot more traffic at the new library after school than at the old building because we were only a few blocks away from the high school; the old library had been a bit of a trek.

Baker loved the kids. He couldn't wait for school to let out and for the teens to come streaming in. During the lull, he liked to camp out by the front door to wait for the first group to come in. When the first few started to show up, he'd escort them over to the reading area so he could jump up onto their books and backpacks and occasionally sit on their homework.

Taylor was shy and a little skittish when there were a lot of adults and teenagers around, but he did like the younger kids. I was always amazed that he let them do things that he'd never let an adult do, like pet his fur the wrong way and let them crawl all over him. He even liked to hang out in the children's section whenever there was a special program going on. One day an author came in to give a talk about dinosaurs and brought in some fossils for the kids to touch. Taylor was right there, mingling with the kids and upstaging the author with his bag of rocks.

I'd sometimes see a toddler who didn't know his ABCs yet try to "read" a book to Taylor. The kid would have a picture book open—more often than not, he was holding it upside down—and Taylor was right there by his side while the kid babbled away, usually something like, "And the cat said meow meow meow." But some of the other kids didn't know what to make of a cat in the library. They'd be reading and suddenly glance over at the corner of the room, and oh no, there was a cat. Other toddlers would see Taylor, look away, then do a double take and really stare. I could almost see the thought bubbles over their heads: *That isn't really a cat, it's a figment of my imagination,* or *That stuffed animal looks a lot like a real cat.* But some didn't want to get too close to find out. Instead, they would try to make a quick getaway, skulking around the perimeter of the room in much the same way Taylor did when he wanted to make a quiet but hasty retreat.

I found out that some kids actually steered clear of the cats because they were afraid of any animal, even a stuffed one. I was surprised that for a ranching community, there were so many kids whose parents did not want animals at home. In time, however, I saw a few of these reluctant kids grow more comfortable being around the cats. And among those who weren't afraid of animals, some would visit the library more frequently just so they could spend time with the cats, who were basically their surrogate pets.

There was one high school student who came in almost every day to do his homework after school, and Baker liked to hang out with him because the kid wrote with one hand while petting Baker with the other. "The minute I graduate, I'm going to leave home and go out and get as many cats and dogs as I can," he told me once.

Taylor also liked the evening story times that children's librarian Carol Nageotte would hold about once a month. She'd set up the children's library like a living room, with a rocking chair and stuffed animals, and spread a quilt out onto the floor so the kids could settle in to listen to the stories. They'd bring their own stuffed animals and wear their pajamas—some of the parents would, too—and even Carol wore a robe and bunny slippers. Taylor usually joined them so he could listen along.

Baker didn't care for story time, but he did like to hang out in Carol's office, which was always a huge mess of costumes and stuffed toys. He'd root around in there and then paw a few things into a nest before settling in for a long afternoon nap. He also liked to hide in the pile when it was time to close the library and we had to put the cats in the workroom for the night. Whenever we couldn't find him, it was the first place we looked, and we were usually successful.

When it came time to tuck the cats in for the night, most of the time Taylor didn't give us much trouble; he liked to get ready for bed on his own without anyone telling him what to do. But Baker could be a little more problematic, as he liked his freedom. So if he wasn't hiding in the children's room, we'd check to see if anyone had shut him up into the meeting room, or if he was fast asleep between a row of books on the shelves.

Once we actually lost Baker. We couldn't find him anywhere. We called him, but we knew that was in vain since they were not cats who came running when you said, "Here, kitty, kitty, kitty." If they felt like it, they'd come, but if and when that happened, they never ran but just calmly strolled right on over, and always in a way to let you know, *Well, I was going to do that anyway.*

Everybody else had gone home, and my fellow librarian Dan Doyle and I had stayed behind to look for him; while Baker was nowhere to be seen, Taylor sat on his afghan in the workroom looking quite virtuous. Once we had exhausted all the usual spots, we started to check behind desks and opened drawers. We finally found him underneath the circulation desk sleeping quite cozily in one of the cupboards.

"Baker!" Dan scolded him. "We were calling for you, why didn't you respond?"

"Why should he?" I answered for him as I scooped him up and headed for the workroom. "After all, he was right where he wanted to be."

The only time they fought me was when they had to go to the vet, because it combined the two things they hated more than anything in the world: leaving the library and getting in a car. The only way to get them into the cat carriers was with brute force: I opened the door of the carrier, took hold of the back end, and somehow maneuvered the rest of the body in while the cat fought the good fight. Once we were at the vet's office, of course then he pulled a one-eighty and didn't want to come out: I'd open the door, upend the carrier, and then attempt to decant the cat while he braced himself against the sides of the carrier so he could stay in.

We all began to dread it so much that the vet, Dr. Bob Gorrindo, actually wrote out a prescription for Valium, which read as follows:

RX: Library Cats. ¼ tablet by mouth. 2 mg. May cause drowsiness. Do not drink alcohol. Keep out of reach of children.

In fact, both Baker and Taylor became very nervous whenever they had to do anything that wasn't part of their normal everyday routine. And they liked to stay indoors; they were not at all curious about the outside world. Maybe a month after Baker arrived, a patron who hadn't yet gotten the memo that there was now a cat living in the library saw him wandering around the stacks and thought he was one of the neighborhood cats that occasionally loitered around outside the library. We were well familiar with them; I think they realized that Baker had a pretty cushy job compared to theirs.

There was one cat named Dudley who hung around for about a year. Even though he already had a home he definitely had his eye on Baker's post as he wandered around outside, moaning and carrying on like he was some poor little homeless cat. Some patrons probably figured we had two already, so what was one more? Anyway, somebody would push him in the front door when we weren't looking, and when we spotted Dudley we'd quickly escort him out the back door. Finally, his owner moved away and took Dudley with him.

So when the patron saw Baker wandering around inside the library, he obviously thought he was doing us a favor by opening a window and putting him outside.

Of course the patron didn't think to tell us, but a couple of times over the course of the morning we heard some faint tapping here and there around the library, but thought nothing of it. Then sometime toward noon, another patron came up to the circ desk.

"I think your cat is outside," he said.

As it turned out, Baker had spent at least an hour or two banging on the window to come back in.

LIBRARY CAT PROFILE: TOBER

Tober arrived at the Thorntown Public Library in Thorntown, Indiana. He has his own blog at The Adventures of Tober, the Thorntown Library Cat (tobersadventures .blogspot.com) where he's attracted an international following due to his celebrity status as the cover cat on the 2014 Baker & Taylor Calendar.

1) *How did you end up living at the library?*

I was rescued by Library Director Karen Niemeyer. At first she tried keeping me as a house cat, but I did *not* like living with her other animals, so she moved me into the library where I was soon promoted to Boss.

2) *What are some of your jobs at the library?*

I like to think of myself as a goodwill ambassador with a little bit of night watchman thrown in. I am great at hunting and killing any bugs that make it into the library. I'm the highlight of most library tours.

3) *What are some of your pet peeves about your job?*

My biggest pet peeve is that all of my employees go home at the end of the day! But I make the most of that time by getting into trouble. I love to eat Post-it notes and sticker paper, silk flowers and Ethernet cords. It's hard to eat those things while the staff is watching. I also don't like it when my dinner is late. Or when staff ignore my requests for treats. Or being upside-downed. Or being locked out of the meeting rooms during an interesting program. Or when my photographer uses the flash on the camera.

4) *Who are some of your favorite patrons, and why?*

I don't think I can name just one favorite patron! My littlest visitors are sometimes the scariest. They are so excited to see me that they make a lot of noise and smash-pet me, which I do not like one bit. But my library people make sure to teach them how to properly approach and pet a cat, so I actually look forward to seeing a lot of little patrons whom I used to run away from!

5) *What's your favorite book?*

Right now one of my favorites is *Miss Hazeltine's Home for Shy and Fearful Cats* by Alicia Potter and Birgitta Sif. It shows how even very small and shy cats (and people, too, I bet) can do very brave things. I also like *Here Comes the Easter Cat* by Deborah Underwood and Claudia Rueda.

6) Do you have advice for other library cats?

Staff training is the key to successful *librarycatdomhood*. Start off on the right paw by making your expectations known to the library director (who will initially think that he or she is Boss, but this notion can be dispelled quickly). Also, if you want extra "people time" at closing, let yourself be "accidentally" locked in a small room overnight, but just once. This will train the humans to look for the cat each night before they close the library. This means extra attention! To make things even more fun, find an unusual place to nap right around closing time. Librarians love the challenge of searching the whole library, including restrooms, storage areas, and offices, to find the sleeping cat!

7) Do you have any advice for librarians who'd like to add a cat to their staff?

Do it! But remember that all of us cats have different personalities and you'll want to get us acclimated to our jobs accordingly. I appreciated being a library office cat before I became a full-blown Library Cat. I got to know my staff better this way and I was gradually introduced to the rest of the library. I'm also very polite and nonconfrontational, so I have lots of quiet spots I can visit when things get too busy or loud. My coworkers love having me around, and I love the seat-warming they do. Also, they're great for getting treats out of drawers for me. And belly rubs! The belly rubs are great!

8) Anything else you'd like to add?

Being a Library Cat is one of the best jobs in the whole world. If you are a cat and you have the opportunity to become a Library Cat, go for it! (Just don't nap in the book return. Dangerous!)

FOUR

For the first few months after the cats arrived, I think I spent too much time on the cats and not enough time on my job. Then again, I think all of us did.

One day, I was petting Taylor with one hand while typing a letter with the other. "You know, I think the cats really cut down on our productivity," Constance remarked.

I grunted and continued to type. Even though we had been in the new library for almost a year, we were still playing catch-up because of all the time it took to set everything up, then adjusting to a new location for everything as well as hiring a few new staff members.

"I mean, think about it," she said. "At least several times a day, I'm taking time out of my schedule to pet one of the cats—or both—talk to them, and then chat about them with others. But it can't help but have a softening effect, for both staff and patrons." She paused. "I think they've softened you up a bit as well."

"Well, it's nice to finally go to work and have somebody around who likes me," I replied.

I was only half kidding. Not only was I the librarian in charge of collecting and recording library fines, but I was not one to smile with great frequency. As a child, it just didn't come naturally to me, and four decades later, not much had changed.

I think we were all surprised at how fast the cats adapted to life in a library. It became apparent to us very quickly that they were always curious about whatever we were doing, and they liked to be "helpful." If Baker was sitting on a desk and there was a pencil or paper clip within paw's reach, he'd flick it onto the floor, as if to say, *This was in your way,* though I always thought he really did it to make more room for himself to sprawl out. So very early on, I learned to be neat around my desk and actually gathered up a pile of rocks I could put on top of various stacks of paper.

But I had to admit, Constance was right. Spending your working hours alongside a couple of cats—regardless of whether they spent most of the time sound asleep—was comforting. And if something or someone made you really mad, there was nothing like a nice purring feline to help you calm down. While they weren't sit-on-your-lap cats, just having them within arm's reach—or indeed, knowing they were somewhere in the library—was enough.

She was also correct in that the cats were responsible for eating up a lot of our time in a different way. Because it was so unusual to have cats living in a public library, we spent a lot more time talking and interacting with patrons than we did before. After all, we had to sell the cats to the general public.

And so, instead of just stamping books and adding up fines owed, we took time to answer patrons' questions and tell them about the breed. We were very proud of the cats as well as our new library.

Baker and Taylor also made it close to impossible to make a quick run to the grocery store. I already knew that living in a small town meant that the simple act of grabbing a carton of milk and paying for it could turn into an hour-long detour as I ran into friends, acquaintances, and patrons, and we asked after each other and made the obligatory small talk. After the cats arrived, that time easily doubled as people asked about the cats as soon as they spotted me, regardless of whether they'd been in the library a week ago or just that morning.

Constance was also right about how the cats were softening me up. So I did something that was rarely witnessed at the library: I smiled.

And she smiled back.

⸻

About a month after Taylor arrived, a professional photographer showed up at the library so we could keep our end of the bargain with Bill Hartman and Baker & Taylor. We scheduled the photo shoot for a Sunday, when the library was closed. It was already clear that the cats hated to travel—one short drive to the vet had already proven that—so I told Bill it would be easier for all involved if we could set everything up at the library. Fortunately, he agreed.

Yvonne and I watched as the photographer arranged the lights and cameras and a huge roll of paper which would serve as the background. A few of the staff came in on their day off to watch as well. The cats stayed in the workroom until the photographer was ready.

When the photographer signaled it was time to begin, we opened the door, and in keeping with his normal schedule, Baker immediately headed over to his favorite sunny spot at the end of the stacks. When I herded him over to the set he gave me a look that said, *What are you doing?* but he stayed close. He was particularly interested in the backdrop, and kept walking behind it to see if we were hiding anything there. Taylor, on the other hand, sauntered right over to the circulation desk, leaned his back against it, and promptly arranged himself into his Buddha position.

The photographer frowned. "He can't sit like that for the photos, you can see his private parts."

Hmmm . . . Maybe this wasn't going to be as easy as I thought; I assumed the photographer would snap a few rolls of film and then we'd all go out to lunch. "Well, that's how he sits," I explained.

Bill nodded. "I think it's best if he sits like a normal cat."

Bill was one of my favorite people in the world. After all, he was the reason why we now had two cats roaming around the library.

"Easier said than done," I said, which would apply to the entire session. But luckily, after we placed the cats on the backdrop, Taylor sat like a regular cat, and the photographer snapped away while Yvonne and I stood off to the side of the camera jumping, squealing, and waving our hands to get the cats to look up, look down, and tilt their heads in a certain way. All was well for about five minutes, but then both cats decided that they simply didn't want to be in that spot anymore or sit that way, so Baker started to walk away while Taylor went into Buddha mode and calmly—and meticulously—proceeded to clean himself.

I stopped jumping around and the photographer stepped away from his camera. It looked like it was going to be a long day.

"Do you have any props or toys?" the photographer asked.

"Wait a minute," I said, and ran to the workroom to get a few of their toys. When I returned, I saw that one of the photographer's assistants had given them a few treats, which kept them in place for a minute or two. We took our places again as the assistant brushed a few crumbs from the backdrop. I held a ball that rattled in one hand and a feather on the end of a stick in the other. I stood off to the side shaking them while I danced around a little; the photographer madly snapped away. As before, five minutes seemed to be the cats' limit before their attention spans wavered and they wandered off yet again.

We herded them back onto the backdrop and I immediately formed a makeshift conga line, grabbing anyone I could.

This time, a whole two minutes passed before Baker stood up and shook himself off, as if to say, *Okay, I've had enough.* He marched off the backdrop, this time with Taylor in his wake.

While I was embarrassed that the cats were, well, acting like cats, the photographer didn't seem to mind. We continued on in this vein for a couple of hours: five minutes on, ten minutes off, while I twisted myself into a pretzel to help the cats respond and not make them freak out any more than was absolutely necessary.

"We need something else," the photographer said after about the seventeenth break.

I shook the feather boa in his face. "Like this?"

"No, something to put in the shot that they like and that looks good against the backdrop but doesn't upstage them." He looked around the room and I followed his gaze. Books, chairs, file folders. Your typical library. For me, the cats were enough, anything else would just clutter up the photo, I thought.

"What do they like aside from their beds and food bowl?" he asked.

"Give me a minute," I said, and headed back to the work-room to survey the possibilities. Someone had brought in a shopping bag last week, the fancy paper kind that came from a department store. Most cats like to crawl into bags, and Baker had been checking it out this morning.

I grabbed the bag and brought it to the photographer. "How about this?" When I shook it, both cats immediately snapped to attention.

"Let's see." He set the bag on the backdrop, and as expected, Baker and Taylor got to work, sniffing and pawing it and crawl-ing inside. While Baker got his head caught in one of the handles Taylor wriggled inside and peered out at me, blinking.

The photographer grinned and resumed happily snapping away. But soon, I could tell that the cats were getting a little testy because Baker's eyes had narrowed and Taylor's fur was starting to stand on end. The cats looked as if they were just about to wander off again when I thrust my arm into the air and snapped my fingers. "Baker! Taylor! Look here!"

And that's when I accidentally knocked over one of the photographer's lamps. I didn't mean to; I just wanted the whole thing to be over with. I was tired, the cats were tired, and I couldn't help thinking they could find *one* good photograph from the hundreds of shots already taken. At that point, I'd seen so many flashing lights that I'd still be seeing them tomorrow morning.

Baker and Taylor looked up just as the light stand crashed to the floor, which we'd later realize was the exact moment when the photographer snapped the iconic shot that would turn out to be the first poster to feature the cats.

And then they took off.

I was mortified that I broke the light, but the photographer shrugged it off and told me that this kind of thing happens a lot with animals on a shoot and that he totally understood that it was a stressful occasion.

But what worried me more was what would happen if no decent photo came out of all that work. I worried Baker & Taylor would see that the photos turned out horribly and they'd want us to give Taylor back or at least refund their money. Of course it was way too late for that, we were all hooked on the cats and had seen the way they changed the library in such a short time. I vowed to keep them even if I had to find a second, part-time job to pay back the money.

The photographer started to pack up his camera and the assistant took down the backdrop. Was it over?

"I got some great photos," the photographer called on his way out the door.

I found two very cranky cats hiding under the circ desk and herded them into the workroom where they could eat something, and return to an activity that they clearly preferred to posing for cameras: sleeping.

FIVE

Here we go again.

Some people obviously never got the memo that a library is supposed to be a quiet oasis.

A raucous burst of laughter in a library is a real pain when you're trying to get some work done. And it was far from a rare occurrence at the library. In fact, it happened so often that I got pretty good at predicting the exact order of events.

First came several pointed glares, usually delivered by several pairs of eyes peering over the tops of reading glasses.

The offenders would respond with a few muffled apologies and hand waves. But a few minutes later, decorum was once again tossed out the door as a series of laughs that ranged from staccato bursts to ululating trills pierced the still air of the library.

Even Baker's ears twitched.

Again, promises of silence were extended, but as soon as things settled down, once again . . .

HAHAHAHAHAHAHAHAHAHAHA!!!

Then a chorus of "Sorry!"s.

By that point, of course, it was too little too late for the guilty parties.

A heavy and audible sigh was quickly followed by the thump of a chair on the carpeted floor, as the protestor approached the small knot of offenders.

Which would be, uh, *us.*

I was holding court at the circ desk and just finishing up a story about how I had fallen into the dead-animal pit at the county dump. Living in a ranching community meant that sooner or later you had to deal with the occasional dead animal, your own or someone else's. Most ranchers buried them on their property, but some brought them to the dump.

Over the weekend, one of my father's older rams had died, and I'd helped load him into the truck. Once we got to the dump, Dad climbed into the bed of the truck and pushed while I grabbed the legs and pulled. The ram was a pretty good size and wasn't budging, so both of us pushed and pulled harder. Suddenly the body came free and knocked me right into the pit.

I stunk to high heaven, so my father made me ride in the back of the truck on the way home. When we got home, he parked in the barnyard where I had to strip down and get hosed off before he let me go in the house. The yard faced the street, and it seemed like the entire town chose that moment to drive by.

I had just finished that part of the story when the irate patron reached the desk to glare at us. "Come on, ladies, can you please pipe down? I'm trying to get some work done."

We promised to keep it down, but before he sat back down,

Constance cracked, "Sounds like the town got quite a show," and once again we were off and running. The patron threw us one last withering look before he gathered up his books and stormed out of the library.

We viewed our time at the circ desk as a kind of social hour. After all, it was a chance for us to catch up on the gossip around town, rave about a new book, and spend some quality one-on-one time with Baker. It would start when somebody told a joke or related some funny thing that had happened over the weekend, and then all bets were off. Most of us had very distinctive, boisterous laughs. We'd be laughing away and then someone would try to top the joke, and ah, forget it.

It was no secret around town that the Minden branch of the Douglas County Library was far from the typical library, and not just because we had a couple of cats living there full-time. More than a few patrons had commented that the library reminded them of *Cheers,* the old sitcom set in a Boston bar, not because we knew everyone's name—even though we did—but because we were filled with characters. And instead of us shushing the patrons, nine times out of ten it was the patrons who had to tell us to be quiet.

We had a lot of fun, but there was also a good amount of hard work going on behind the scenes. There was always more work than hours in the day, and as often as we laughed, tempers could just as easily fray.

Each staff member had an official title, like library technician or cataloger, but we all rotated various responsibilities throughout the library, from working the circulation desk to shelving books, and even weeding out the collection from time to time.

And while some preferred to stay in the back doing paper-work or repairing books, spending a few hours manning the circ desk could be a definite relief, especially when things got tense in the workroom where we had our desks set up. Every so often, a staffer would be unhappy about something and would either complain or go totally silent. More often, however, somebody else would be humming. Or singing.

Or both.

One staffer named Charlene Cutler worked as a cataloger; her primary job was to type up a card for each new book that came into the library. And she liked to sing . . . a *lot*. Constance, on the other hand, preferred to hum, though most of the time I don't think she was even aware that she was doing it. She usually didn't hum any tune in particular, just a few random notes. Maybe it was just too quiet in the workroom, or maybe they did it to drown out Taylor's snores, but between the singing and humming, sometimes it drove me a little nuts.

But that was only part of it. Charlene chose her songs according to the kind of book she was cataloging. For instance, if she happened to be typing up a card for a book on a patriotic subject, she'd suddenly start belting out "It's a Grand Old Flag," or if she was cataloging a romance novel or a book about relationships, she'd launch into "Let Me Call You Sweetheart." That was in one corner of the workroom; from the other side I'd hear Constance humming, "Hmm, hmm, hmm."

Of course, then Dan wouldn't be able to keep himself from singing along, so he'd pitch in, adding harmony to Charlene's melody. Finally, Constance would stop humming and start singing, too. At that point, I totally gave up hope of getting any work done, and I'd head to the circ desk to volunteer for duty, which of course presented its own social challenges, given the wide variety of people who walked through the door each day. But those challenges were usually short-lived: if a patron was being demanding or difficult, I could help them calm down, find an answer to their question, and they'd be on their way.

Most of the time, the staff got along with each other pretty well, but as is the case in any workplace, you could love your coworkers to pieces, but they could drive you nuts at times.

Of course, I was fully aware that *I* could drive people a little nuts as well.

Dan Doyle came on board at the library in the mid-1980s, and his enthusiasm about everything from books to Russian history—his passion—was contagious. Patrons loved him because he'd bend over backward to help them find something all the while gushing knowledge about the subject . . .

. . . which sometimes included *me*. As a result, Dan has never hesitated to inform any and all comers that I have the disposition of a burnt marshmallow—hard and crusty on the outside and soft and mushy on the inside. Well, I'll just let him describe me.

"Jan could be a little bit of a bear and very much a curmudgeon, but she was like everyone's mother to the staff and tucked us under her wings," he said. "She could be grumpy at times but she had a lot of love underneath so we tended to ignore that because she was always taking care of us."

❖

Despite the fun we all had, I never lost sight of the fact that I worked in a library, and part of what I loved most about it was that while it was a place for people to gather, it was also a structured environment, which required a certain amount of organization and decorum. Since I was one of the longest-serving veterans of the library at that point—we had added several staff members when the new library opened—I had grown accustomed to having things done in a certain way. However, I didn't want to be regarded as one of those doddering old fools who spouted things like, "In my day, we did it *this* way, and if it was good enough back then, it's good enough today."

At the same time, I also knew what my job was, and if someone got in my way then I suppose I could be a bit stubborn. Anytime you stand by your principles or come down firmly on what you think is the right side, others are going to think of you as overly persistent and just a bit inflexible. But if things panned out all right then I was right. And if things didn't, well then, maybe I was just being stubborn at the wrong time.

But things were changing. And sometimes being stubborn meant disappointing people. Even though the burnt crusty outside of me held firm, the mushy marshmallow underneath was always bothered by it.

This conflict was only exacerbated as more people came to see the cats and I occasionally had to play the bad guy. For instance, patrons and visitors alike always wanted to pick up the cats, and all day long I had to tell them they couldn't. For one thing, neither cat liked to be held, and with Baker, if you held him the wrong way it would hurt him. But also, could you imagine what would happen if four hundred people a day were to pick them up? They'd both look like hairless Chihuahuas, well, maybe Chihuahuas with a little extra padding.

There were also some patrons—and a few staff members—who could have easily done without the cats. Some preferred dogs while others were just indifferent, and a few patrons clearly had a bad case of ailurophobia, or fear of cats. So we spent a lot of time explaining that not one penny of taxpayer revenue went toward their care and upkeep, that Yvonne and I paid for everything out of our own pockets. But some didn't know that, or chose not to believe us. One time, a resident read a newspaper article about the county budget for that year and saw a line item that said "pet. cash." They thought it meant money for the cats—not "petty cash"—and headed straight for the county offices with both barrels blazing. The auditors thought it was hysterically funny, and so did we once they passed along the story.

Another time, someone called animal control to report us because they thought we had mutilated the cats' ears.

There was a murky line as to whether Baker and Taylor were privately owned cats or public cats. In a sense, they were public pets much like the ducks at the park that people liked to feed. Of course, in this day and age, pets are still legally regarded as property even though most people consider them to be cherished family members.

As far as I was concerned, Baker and Taylor belonged to Yvonne and me. But I held primary responsibility for feeding them, cleaning up after them, taking them to the vet, and protecting them. I was a protective mother lioness with them in the same way I had been when raising my two children, who were now full-grown adults. Of course, if they were bothering a patron, I'd take them away, but I would not allow anyone else to do anything to them. By the same token, I wouldn't neglect them because I was responsible for them. I thought it was pretty simple.

———◆·◆———

Like me, the cats were not immune to annoying some of the patrons, intentionally or otherwise. Baker was particularly guilty of this since he spent the vast majority of his time sucking up to them. In that way, I always thought that Baker was more like a dog than a cat, and though we tried not to use the term in front of a patron, we commonly referred to Baker as the Library Slut because he was totally free with his favors; anyone who started to pet him was fair game. He'd sit on people's reading material, finagle himself into large handbags, and throw himself in front of their feet so they couldn't move and were forced to pet him.

Baker's cantaloupe addiction almost got him in trouble one day. I was working the circ desk when a red-faced woman ran out of the meeting room.

"Your cat tried to attack me!" she said breathlessly.

I just stared at her. Those cats are so placid they'd have trouble attacking their own fleas, that is, if they had any.

"Was it the gray and white cat?" I calmly asked.

"Yes!"

"Did you pull his tail?"

"Of course not!"

Hmm. "What were you eating?"

"Fruit salad!" she yelled, clearly becoming impatient with playing Twenty Questions. "What does it matter?"

I already knew the answer, but I asked anyway.

"Did it have cantaloupe in it?"

She looked like she was about to have an aneurysm. "Yes, but I don't know what that has to do with anything!"

I returned to stamping books. "He just wants your cantaloupe," I replied.

"*What!?*"

"Baker loves cantaloupe more than anything else in the world. I doubt very much that he attacked you, he probably just tapped you like this, right?" I reached across and lightly tapped her shoulder.

"Where's your supervisor?"

"You're looking at her."

She sighed angrily and stomped back to the meeting room. A minute later, she headed out of the library muttering something about "those crazy cats."

I peeked into the meeting room just to make sure that Baker hadn't morphed into some big bad attack cat. The woman had abandoned her lunch on the table, and there was Baker calmly munching away, careful to pick out the cantaloupe while ignoring the watermelon and berries. The others continued with their meeting as if a cat munching on cantaloupe was an everyday occurrence.

And in our world, it was.

SIX

One day, just after New Year's in 1984, Bill Hartman showed up at the library with a cardboard tube tucked under his arm. He was grinning ear to ear.

"I have a belated Christmas present for you," he said, handing it to me.

"Is this what I think it is?"

"I wanted you to have the first one."

I was a bit nervous. The photo shoot had been so nerve-racking for everyone involved . . . what if I hated the picture or it made the cats look bad in some way?

I unfurled the poster. Baker and Taylor came over to investigate. The poster showed them sitting in front of the slightly battered shopping bag. They looked regal, smart, and friendly but also slightly reserved. The picture had an overall silvery overtone, which enhanced the cats' colors.

"It's perfect," I said.

"We love it, too," said Bill. "We can't wait to see what librarians think."

"How could anyone not love it?" I said, running my finger over the image of the cats. Baker was about to start chewing on the edge of the poster before I shooed him away.

Bill told me he was headed to the midwinter meeting of the American Library Association in Washington, D.C., a gathering of librarians to meet, learn, and check out forthcoming books, and where Baker & Taylor would debut the poster.

"We'll be shipping a few cartons of posters to give away on the trade-show floor," he explained. "Sometimes we have leftovers to ship back. I think they'll do well, but we don't know."

Based on the oohs and aahs coming from the staff and patrons who had assembled to see the poster, I'd bet money that other librarians would love it, too.

"Too bad you can't come," he said.

Too bad, indeed. There was nothing I loved more than a library convention. Not only did it provide me with a chance to travel to a different part of the country, but I could also get a firsthand look at new books that were coming out over the next few months, go to seminars and workshops where I could pick up a few new ideas, meet up with other librarians, and generally let my hair down. Most patrons would find it hard to believe that their mostly prim and proper library staff could party with the best of them.

As library director, Yvonne got first dibs when it came to attending conventions, but this year it wasn't in the cards for anyone. Even though 1983 had been a great year at the library, first settling into the new building and then dealing with the cats' arrival, the truth is that behind the scenes things were pretty grim, and we all did our best to keep it hidden from patrons.

In January 1984, county legislators had cut the budget for the upcoming fiscal year by fifteen percent across the board for all departments, beginning in July. Essentially that meant that all of us had to work forty hours but only get paid for thirty-two. That was bad enough, but what was worse is that they cut our book budget for the current year in half retroactively, which meant that instead of having $15,500 remaining to buy books for the next six months, a comfortable cushion for a library our size, the decrease left us with just a couple of thousand dollars.

When we got the news, Yvonne became incensed. She closed the door to her office and proceeded to spend the rest of the day on the phone with the county commissioners while the rest of us put on our best faces for patrons. It wasn't easy. Besides budget woes, we were already stretched thin, and asked to do more with less. In the weeks since the bad news, I had noticed that Baker was attracting a lot more attention—and pets—from the staff.

At the time, we were also in the middle of a massive state-wide project where we were converting from using a card catalog to a centralized computer system. Every library in the state was involved, and while the libraries in larger cities had more staff and resources to handle it, the small libraries like ours were struggling in terms of money and staff even before the budget cuts.

Essentially, we had to type in a record for every book on

our shelves. We'd grab a drawer from the card catalog, bring it over to the computer that was hooked up to the statewide network up in Carson City, and just start typing. One card at a time—author, title, subject, date of publication, publisher, page count, Dewey decimal number, ISBN, and so on—over and over again.

Since it was a statewide database, if another library had already typed the record of a certain book into the computer, we had to type in that we also had a copy at our library. But first we had to actually walk over to the stacks to see if it was still there, and that no one had walked off with it or misshelved it. And if it wasn't on the shelf, we then had to go through the cards from books that were already checked out at the circulation desk to verify that it was at somebody's home.

The one advantage was that in 1984, a computer monitor was easily bigger than a microwave oven and threw off just as much heat, which meant it was a perfect place for cats: it was something nice and toasty they could sit on and high enough off the ground so they could look around and survey their kingdom. In other words, during these frequent exercises in frustration, the good news was that a cat was usually never too far away.

I'd sit at the computer, a drawer from the card catalog beside me, as I mentally prepared myself to dive into mind-numbing work when something would start blinking, beeping, or squawking, or else the green cursor would disappear into the black screen. Keep in mind this is years before Windows. Back then computers came with several manuals each the size of a phone book that typically devoted ten single-spaced pages to how to turn the blasted thing on and then boot up with those hideous floppy disks. It was obvious that in the vast majority of cases, engineers and developers were writing them.

I'd reach for one of the manuals and squint at the instructions, which may as well have been written in Esperanto. Fortunately, that's the exact moment when whichever cat was currently lolling on top—usually Baker—would reach out a paw and tap me on the top of the head as if to say, *Hey, what's the problem? Why don't you scratch my head instead?*

They always knew when we needed them most.

At one point, the entire database crashed and about half of the entries were wiped out. Of course somebody had failed to back everything up, which meant that we had to start completely from scratch and reenter everything.

We were supposed to do this in our "spare time," which would have made us laugh uproariously *if* we'd had the time to spare. With a bigger library and more patrons due to the growth in the valley, we were stretched to the limit. We had to recruit more volunteers since the budget cuts also prohibited us from hiring new employees, which we desperately needed. So we had to attend more Friends of the Library meetings and plan more events so we could attract more volunteers, all of which took up even more hours. It was a vicious cycle.

It was certainly an interesting time, which is the same thing people said about World War II.

We tried to keep on top of things, but the entire process took several years and sometimes it was just more work than any of us could cope with. We all ran out of patience at one point or another, and we occasionally became short with patrons, especially when it came time to pay their fines; an extra fifty cents here and there wouldn't have mattered in the grand scheme of things of course, but it was the principle that bothered me. And whenever somebody returned a book that looked like it had been boiled, then microwaved, and finally run through a Cuisinart for good measure, I had to work overtime to hold my tongue.

That's when I'd look around for Baker. Just a minute or two of sinking my fingers into his thick plush coat was enough to take the edge off. That's when I think it really sunk in that the cats made a huge difference.

Along with the computers, the keyboards presented another challenge: after all, it was one more thing we were paying attention to instead of the cats. So if Baker wasn't fast asleep on top of the monitor, he'd hang his head over the edge and watch our fingers fly—or not—across the keyboard. Occasionally I had to nudge a clump of whiskers or a paw out of the way so I could see what I was typing. When he got bored or hungry, he'd reach down and swat at my fingers. And if that didn't work—and if he was in a particularly insistent mood that day—he'd call upon the same skills he employed when he couldn't distract a patron from his newspaper.

He'd jump down onto the keyboard and refuse to move.

"Baker!" I'd scold him, but with a smile as I removed him from the keyboard. Occasionally I'd even let him take a stroll across the keyboard just so I could see what he came up with. Most of the time a mishmash of letters and symbols appeared on the monitor something like this:

FREJIOP345308T5I54690^&()(*&^&$%^#*

But one day it was clear that Baker had something he wanted to say when the following letters appeared on the screen.

HIHIHIHIHIHIHIHIHIHI

"Hello to you, too, Baker," I told him as I scratched his head. "But you still have to move."

❦

During those times, it was a rare day when I didn't cross my fingers and wish that a nice big clump of fur would clog up the computer to give us a break and allow us to catch up on our normal workload. I often dreamed about chucking it all and returning to the good old days when our main tools were our trusty date-due stamps and a pencil eraser. I don't think most people realized how stressful it was to learn to use computers and the tension it created among a staff of mostly older women. After all, back then, home answering machines were still a real novelty, so the mere idea that there was a computer in a library, well, some librarians were threatened by it. We were all old-school, and while some of the old-timers around the county thought that the new library was a total waste of money because they'd never even set foot in the old one, the newcomers, of course, had a different take. They loved the new library, but compared to the cities and large suburban areas of California where most of them had moved from, it wasn't big enough, and neither were the other municipal services Douglas County offered.

People were still coming in droves, and not just for the cats. Baker and Taylor just happened to arrive at a particularly stressful period in Carson Valley history, and the region was quickly becoming home to two different groups of people.

In the early 1980s, Minden and the entire Carson Valley was changing, for good and for bad. The economy was in recession, and many ranchers had no choice but to sell their land and cattle because they couldn't afford to stay in business. As a result, some of their kids couldn't find well-paying jobs in the area, so after the land was gone, they had no choice but to leave. Meanwhile, lots of people from California were moving in. The Carson Valley is filled with multigenerational ranching families who had been here for decades, and the traditional old-timers who made do and newcomers accustomed to more municipal services often clashed.

Though the recent arrivals had moved here for the sheer beauty of the valley as well as the lower cost of living, once they settled in they began to wonder what kind of backwater they had moved to, an impression no doubt helped along by the size of our tiny library, though to us, the new library was the size of a shopping mall compared to the previous building.

The one bright spot, of course, was the cats. After all, their libraries back in California didn't have a resident cat, let alone two, and so even if they walked in the front door of the library ready to complain about the fact that we lacked a certain book and had to wait maybe weeks for us to obtain it from another library through the interlibrary loan program, a quick glimpse of Baker fast asleep on top of the monitor or of Taylor propped up against the circulation desk in his Buddha position helped ease the tension and tempers.

We soon heard back from Bill after the conference. "How'd it go?"

"They loved them," he said. "We ran out of posters the first day. Some even grabbed several to bring home."

"Well, that explains the strange phone calls last week," I said. "And the mail."

"What do you mean?"

The librarians who had made a run on the posters at the Baker & Taylor booth had seen the line on the front that listed the Douglas County Library as the cats' home and were apparently so enamored of the cats that they decided to call us to make sure they were real. And in that day's mail were a few cards and letters addressed to the cats to add to the stack that had already piled up, each one from a librarian or supposedly written by a cat owned by a librarian, though none so far had said they also lived in a library.

The first time I answered one of these calls, both I and the caller were a bit confused.

"Douglas County Library."

"Are Baker and Taylor there?"

"Yes."

"Can I speak to them?"

I was working the circulation desk. Five people were waiting in line to have books checked out, a parade of squealing toddlers and their mothers were heading for the children's section for story time, and out of the corner of my eye I saw a small plume of smoke emerge from the copy machine.

Constance was out sick that day, and I wouldn't put it past her to pull something like this.

"Constance, this isn't funny," I began. "The library is packed, we're short staffed, and—"

There was a pause on the other end. "Who's Constance?" The woman identified herself as a librarian from somewhere in New England who had hung the poster up in her library the day after she returned from the convention, and all her coworkers wanted to know where they could get one of their own.

But first she wanted to say hi to the cats on the phone.

I sighed and held the phone up to Baker, who was sprawled out on the circ desk on a handmade mat—fuzzy fleece on one side, flannel on the other—that an elderly patron had made for him after scolding us, saying that she thought the Formica counter looked like it would be uncomfortable for a cat.

Of course Baker didn't seem to care either way; he just wanted to be able to greet people and it would make it easier for them to rub his belly if he was elevated and easily accessible.

"Say good-bye to your adoring public," I told him after I hung up the phone.

There were five more calls that day: three from librarians who repeated the first librarian's request—other staff members at their library wanted a poster of their own—while two were from reporters from the library trade journals.

It's only temporary, I told myself as I started in on the stack of mail addressed to the cats on my desk. Inside were more requests for posters and mash notes to the cats. A librarian in Las Vegas even enclosed an interlibrary loan request to "borrow" one of the cats with the special request PLEASE DO NOT MAIL IN BOOK BAG. I passed it around to the other staff members, and we all had a good laugh at that. Instead of a cat—real or otherwise—I sent her a poster via regular mail.

In one of the letters, a woman asked for a copy of the poster, but added, "Could you please have them *pawtograph* it?" Like most cats, Baker and Taylor made it clear when they didn't want to be forced to do something, and I thought that mashing one of their paws into an inkpad and then pressing it onto a sheet of paper or a poster fell into that category.

But the letter writer did earn a few brownie points for coining the word "pawtograph," which I thought was rather clever. So I set her note aside, and the next day I brought in a rubber stamp shaped like a pawprint and stamped the poster twice—I made Taylor's a little lighter so as to distinguish the two—using a green inkpad; after all, the library logo was green, as well as our stationery and business cards.

Word of the cats was starting to spread in some unusual places after the first poster came out that spring. On April 24, 1984, the Morgan Hill earthquake struck the San Francisco Bay Area at 6.2 on the Richter scale. The epicenter was near San Jose, and though we felt it in Minden, along with a number of aftershocks, the quake didn't cause any major damage in the Carson Valley. We thought nothing of it when a local reporter called to see if everything was okay.

But the next day, a map appeared on the front page of the *San Francisco Chronicle,* with call-outs showing damage to houses and buildings throughout the region. We were all surprised—and more than a little amused—to see that tiny Minden was included.

"Jolt moves buildings," the call-out read. "Moves local library shelves about a foot, woke up the library cat."

——◅•▻——

In addition to the fan mail, visitors began to show up at the library, a trickle in the early months of 1984 after the first poster came out, but by summer that number had grown to at least five or six each day. On Saturdays, it could be ten or more. It might not sound like a lot, but especially if they'd made a long trip just to see the cats, they wanted to spend some time visiting with them and talking with us, which, again, ate into time that we didn't have, but we couldn't exactly refuse them. Besides, I liked to see how happy the cats made other people, even if they only knew them from a poster hanging on the wall of a library. And it was an opportunity to spread my belief that every library would benefit from having a cat or two on staff.

Sometimes visitors would bring treats, food, and toys for the boys, and sometimes they'd want to see the cats enjoy their gifts right that second. As I've always done whenever a guest brought a bottle of wine to dinner at my house, I accepted it, thanked the giver, and then set it aside for later. If it was food, I'd explain that they'd scarf it all down, and then we'd need to go buy a little stepstool so that they could get on top of the circulation desk because they'd grow so fat.

But the truth is that I never gave any of the edible gifts to the cats, because I never knew for sure what was in them. Besides, a strange food or treat might have been too harsh for their digestive systems.

You could never be too careful.

As part of their service to the community, most public libraries offer a space where groups and nonprofits can meet throughout the year, from the local historical society to a foreign
language club. We knew how important it was to have a comfortable space, and had spent many a late night working out
the details with the architect when planning the new library.
Happily, the meeting room was extremely popular, and besides the fact that we were open late at night, we also didn't
charge a fee to use it like other buildings and organizations
in town.

One of my new responsibilities was to book the meeting
room and keep track of the schedule; at times, it was like cho-
reographing a year-long ballet. At the beginning of each new
year, I called every group that met regularly, from once a week
to once a month, and put them on the schedule. The rest of the
time, if it wasn't already booked anyone could use it.

The cats loved to wander into the room during the day if the
door was open. When I was sitting at my desk down the hall, it
was not uncommon to hear a group of monotone, low-pitched
voices suddenly erupt into a bunch of squeals and giggles.

One of the cats must have just walked in, I thought.

In March 1984, a year after Baker first arrived at the library,
reporters and columnists were already referring to the pair as
"nationwide celebrities."

Within six months after the first poster came out, all thirty
thousand copies were out of stock, and librarians and book-

stores were clamoring for more, but since the company had decided not to reprint the first poster it became something of a collector's item. James Brooke, a marketing director at Baker & Taylor at the time, was flooded with requests. "It's nice to know Baker and Taylor are doing a good job of promoting us, but I'm getting tired of my office looking like the mailroom," he told me in a letter. "Despite the fact that we've distributed posters and shopping bags seemingly to every library in the world, we still get a steady stream of requests for Baker and Taylor items. It's obvious that these cats are the two most popular animals in the country."

A year after Baker and Taylor had arrived, none of us—staff or patrons—could imagine life without the cats.

LIBRARY CAT PROFILE: LOUIE

Louie is a brown tabby cat who works at the Freedom Public Library in Freedom, New Hampshire. On April Fool's Day in 2009, his human colleagues stuck a bar code on his head and posted a photo online with the headline "Check Out Louie (April Fool!)." Louie did not appreciate the humor.

1) *How did you end up living at the library?*

I don't really "live" at the library, but I go to work every day when the library is open since it is right across the street from my house. I live with the library director, Elizabeth, and I always try to be there when the library is open.

2) *What are some of your jobs at the library?*

My main job is to sit at the circulation desk and greet patrons. On nice days, I'll sit on the sidewalk outdoors and speak to everyone as they pass. Sometimes, I'll hang out in the children's room if someone wants to read out loud to me, and after movies and films I'll clean up the dropped popcorn from the floor.

3) *What are some of your pet peeves about your job?*

The library can be busy. Sometimes when it becomes too crowded at the circulation desk it becomes difficult for people to pet me. I sometimes have to walk over stacks of books or DVDs in order for everyone to be able to reach me.

4) *Who are some of your favorite patrons, and why?*

I love everybody, really. Our regular volunteers know me very well and they help watch out for me. And I enjoy Wednesday morning story time when the library is full of families. I especially like the summer residents who return to Freedom seasonally. For many of them, one of the first things they do when they get here is visit me at the library. I look forward to seeing how much kids have grown from year to year.

5) *What is your favorite book?*

I've always liked Sara Swan Miller's *Three Stories You Can Read to Your Cat* and *Three More Stories You Can Read to Your Cat*. I also enjoy anything that Elizabeth reads at home in bed where I can curl up on her chest with the open book.

6) *Do you have advice for other library cats?*

Remember that you're an ambassador for reading and libraries. Sometimes people come to the Freedom Public Library just to meet me and they end up becoming a regular patron.

7) *Do you have any advice for librarians who'd like to add a cat to their staff?*

When I'm at work we keep a sign on the outside door saying I'm inside. That way, if there's someone who can't be around me, or if someone wants to bring their dog inside, I can go out another door without making a big deal out of it.

8) *Anything else you'd like to add?*

Time for dinner. I better go home.

SEVEN

From the first day I started working at the library and even more so after the cats arrived on the scene, it felt like I had stepped right back into my childhood: I was surrounded by books and animals. The two had provided me with stability and comfort for as long as I could remember.

I was born on August 19, 1931, and grew up in the Piedmont section of Oakland, California. My maternal grandmother lost everything in the crash of 1929, and the only thing left was a Craftsman-style home designed by the renowned architect Bernard Maybeck. Several generations lived together in the house perched on a hill overlooking San Francisco Bay. One of my earliest memories is watching the original Bay Bridge from Oakland to San Francisco being built.

Despite the fact that I grew up during the Depression and World War II, my childhood was a very happy one. My family on both sides was an intriguing collection of go-getters and misfits, some of quite famous lineage, but eccentrics all. On my mother's side, my uncle Harry Cobden had played an instrumental role in inventing the Quonset hut, helped preserve an eight-hundred-acre parcel in Big Sur from development, and spent various stints as a rodeo cowboy, spy, and Golden Gloves boxer. On my father's side, my paternal great-grandfather Henry H. Haight served as governor of California from 1867 to 1871, and is generally regarded to be the namesake "Haight" in Haight-Ashbury. My father was also a direct descendant of Commodore John Paty, who helped to discover the northern Hawaiian Islands and served as a confidant of King Kamehameha in the mid-1800s.

My book-loving side traces back to a few literary-minded relatives who preceded me: my aunt Charlotte Cobden Jackson wrote and edited children's books and served as children's book editor for the *San Francisco Chronicle*. She was married to Joseph Henry Jackson, who was literary editor at the *Chronicle* from 1930 to 1955 and served as John Steinbeck's editor for a time.

My parents loved to tell stories about all of them. Early on, I got the message that my brother Tony—two years younger— and I came from strong stock, and that we should strive to do great things, too. But all I wanted to do was read and spend time with animals, and if I could do both at the same time, so much the better.

Fortunately, both were always close at hand during my childhood. My parents were devoted dog people: if it barked and wagged a tail, it was acceptable. Cats, not so much.

In keeping with family tradition, even our pets were eccentric. We had a long line of canine housemates through the years, including a black sausage-shaped dog of uncertain ancestry who showed up at the house one day and never left. My parents named him Piggy, and we quickly discovered that he was partial to stealing open bottles of beer from anyone who momentarily released their grasp. Piggy would chug down the contents and then clamber upstairs so he could perform his favorite game in the world: carpet-surfing down the hall that ran the length of the house.

After getting a running head start, Piggy would land on one end of the carpet runner, which he'd "surf" until the carpet stopped moving toward the end of the hall. He'd hop off and wait until someone came along to straighten out the carpet, usually accompanied by the lament, "Oh, Piggy!" A minute or so later, he'd do it all over again, which would go on all afternoon, at least until the dog sobered up.

Piggy was only one of a herd of animals I loved in my childhood. The neighborhood also held a wide assortment of dogs, cats, birds, you name it, and I spent countless hours playing with them until my worried parents came calling for me. If my parents didn't find me hanging out with the neighbors' pets, they knew to head for the library.

My fate was forever sealed when I was seven years old and got my first library card at the branch library off Piedmont Avenue a few blocks away.

I already knew how to read, and had plowed through my own collection of books so often I could recite them from memory. So armed with my new library card, I started at the beginning of the children's section, reading every book on the shelf in alphabetical order starting with *A*. I'd take a whole section of books and plop down on the floor to read. Most of the time, I was so engrossed in the stories I was reading that I didn't notice when other patrons had to step over me. I also didn't hear the librarian's heavy sighs over me being the last one in the library and if only I would go home then she could close up early. However, I did detect that she had started to frown whenever she saw me walk through the door.

When it was time for the library to close, I'd count out ten books from my stack—which was the limit each patron could check out at one time—and put the others back on the shelf. I'd then carry all ten books up to the desk, my little arms struggling to contain them all, where the librarian tapped her fingers on her desk and glared at me.

The next day, I'd bring them all back and dive right back into the stacks, picking up where I had left off.

One night, as the librarian stamped my books with a heavier hand than usual, she gave me a note and told me to give it to my mother. After she read it, my mother told me that from that point on, I could only check out five books a night from the library. At first I didn't understand; to me, that's what a library was for, so people could check out books. But I figured that either the librarian didn't want to reshelve so many books or she wanted to cut out early.

I protested, but not too much, since my mother wanted to keep the peace. I still went to the library every afternoon after school and the librarian still glowered at me, but I had already lined up other sources to draw on. After all, I read all the time, night and day, and like any good addict, I always had to know where my next fix was coming from.

Kelton Court, where we lived, was a cul-de-sac of massive houses. Nobody locked their doors back then, so I considered the books in the neighbors' houses to be part of my own personal library. The family across the street lived in a big Spanish Colonial house and had a complete collection of the original L. Frank Baum Oz books stored in their garage. The first time I saw them, I almost fainted; at the time, they were my holy grail.

No one was ever home during the day, and judging from the dead rats floating in the fountain in their courtyard, they had bigger problems to deal with, so I figured, why bother them? Besides, I always brought the books back when I was done.

The woman next door knew I loved to read, so one day she invited me into her house and brought me up into an octagon-shaped tower room with big windows looking out onto the Bay and wooden benches that ran all the way around the perimeter. She lifted up the top of one of the benches and gestured for me to take a look.

Inside were hundreds of children's books, and that was just one bench. She said I could come over and read any time I wanted. I started that day. I'd lie down on the bench and read until it got so dark that I couldn't see the words or when I heard my mother calling, whichever came first.

I almost didn't have to go to the Piedmont library anymore, but I did because I hadn't yet finished reading all the books in the children's section, and a tiny part of me realized that my presence would annoy the librarian.

After I'd read all the children's books at the library and the neighbors' houses, I started in on the adult books in our house, like *In Darkest Africa* by Teddy Roosevelt. Many of these books had belonged to my grandfather when he was a student at Yale, back in the early 1900s. It didn't matter if they were about big game hunting or the law, I read them because they were there.

◦•◦

My parents both worked full-time for most of my childhood. During the Depression, my father had a job working in the sewers and Mother worked as a salesgirl-model at an Oakland department store. My mother was like Auntie Mame, and she even looked a little like Rosalind Russell. She wasn't fond of either housework or cooking, and knew only two settings on the stove: off and high.

So it was left to me to do a lot of the housework and watch my younger brother, Tony. I was a lot bigger than him; when I was twelve years old, I was five feet ten and the tallest kid in the class, boys included. Tony was pretty scrawny and some of the kids in the neighborhood liked to pick on him.

One day after school, I was reading a book in the front yard when Tony came home crying.

"Herbie Hagen hit me and he said he's going to hit me again tomorrow," he said.

I stood up, still reading the book. "Where's Herbie?"

"Up at the other end of the street," he sniffled.

"Okay, let's go." I stuck out the hand that wasn't holding the book, which he grabbed and led the way so I could continue to read without tripping on the sidewalk. When we reached Herbie, Tony stopped and I lowered the book. With my free hand I punched him in the nose.

"Don't you ever touch him again!" I told Herbie, and raised the book back up in front of my face. Tony again took my hand and led me back toward home. It had occurred to me to hit him with the book because it would have probably hurt more, but I didn't want to damage a book on stinky old Herbie Hagen. Besides, it was a library book and the mean librarian would probably fine me if I returned it with blood on it.

I also had to take care of the house, though I wasn't that good at it, probably because I spent most of the time when I wasn't in school reading. My mother's favorite phrase during the day was "How about you dust?" while at night it was "You're going to ruin your eyes," given the countless times she told me to turn off the light and go to sleep. I always complied without a fight because I kept a stash of flashlights handy so I could read under the covers.

A few weeks before Christmas in 1941, I decided to give my mother a break and finally do some dusting. I started in my mother's bedroom and had turned on the radio so I could listen to some music to help pass the time. Suddenly, the music stopped. A man with a very serious voice came on to announce that Pearl Harbor had just been attacked, and I ran downstairs to tell everyone. I knew our lives had just changed, but I didn't know how.

Within a matter of weeks, our world was in upheaval. My father was drafted into the Marines and my mother started working at the Naval Supply Depot at the Port of Oakland, where she was an assistant to Admiral Chester W. Nimitz.

Before my father reported for duty, he worked as an air raid warden in the East Bay. He was very strict about turning off every single light in the house whenever the sirens went off or when there was a mandatory blackout in effect. We all had to trudge down to the basement, which I hated because it was not only pitch-black but filled with mice, both dead and alive.

There were a couple of cabin-shaped mousetraps to help cut down on the vermin, but that didn't make me feel any better. One night my pigtail got caught in the mouse mausoleum and my father refused to turn on the light so I could get my hair out of there. After that, whenever the sirens blared and we had to run downstairs, I always begged my parents to stay upstairs, but it was to no avail.

Everything was rationed, from meat to clothes. Paper was also rationed, which meant there weren't many new books being published, but I didn't mind, I just read what was available. As long as it had print on a page, I didn't care if it was old or new, or if I had already read it for that matter.

My housework responsibilities had tripled, but in between cleaning and taking care of my little brother, I still managed to spend most of my day with my nose in a book.

Everything was so uncertain; we didn't know what the future was going to look like, if the entire Bay Area would get bombed into oblivion or if we'd have to start speaking German or Japanese.

Finally, after four long years, the war was over, but some things didn't really change much. My parents were still working full-time while I kept reading and tried to remember to dust every so often.

I attended Ursuline, a Catholic high school for girls in Santa Rosa, for three years. I worked part-time in the library there, which consisted of only one tiny room, but I couldn't believe my great fortune. To me the best job in the world would be to work in a library where no one could ever tell me I was reading too many books. The mother superior also loved books and she'd come into the library and say hello to me.

Then she'd pick up a book and start rubbing the cover, almost as if it were a cat. "This is a good book," she'd say as she continued to stroke it.

The nuns packed our schedule to the hilt so I didn't have much time to read. At least once a day we were required to walk around a circular driveway in front of the school while we recited the rosary. After we were done we could keep walking if we liked, and most girls did just so they could put off doing their homework for as long as possible.

I stayed out there too, but for a different reason: so I could read. After all, I had lots of practice walking and reading with Tony while I defended him against the neighborhood bullies. As a result, I could walk and read rings around the other girls.

After graduation, I took a few classes at the University of California in Berkeley. I also took a part-time job at the East Asiatic library at the university, and even though I couldn't read any of the books there, it really didn't matter. I was working in a library, surrounded by books. What else could I need?

I started hanging out with a crowd who fancied themselves to be the beatniks of the day, including Mort Sahl, who would later become a famous comedian and political satirist. We all hung out at Throckmorton Hall on Shattuck Avenue, and I soon took a fancy to a graduate student I'd met, and he to me. People were trying to push the memory of the atrocities of World War II far into the past, which meant looking forward as much as possible. We figured there was no real reason to wait to get married and so within a year of our first meeting I had become the wife of an aspiring professor of philosophy.

We moved into a small apartment at 2214A Carlton Street not far from campus. The rent was only $37 a month and part of the deal was that we had to take care of a cat named 22, short for the address. We knew we'd be heading to England shortly so my husband could study at Cambridge University, and since I missed being surrounded by the animals in Piedmont, any indignity I felt at calling out, "Time for dinner, 22!" was eased by the fact that there was an animal there at all.

We headed to England in 1952 and settled into daily life in Conington, a small village outside Cambridge. It was shocking to see bombing debris that hadn't been cleared away yet and much of the country still looked like a war zone. I was fine with the strict rationing, from meat and eggs to fuel and clothing, since I had helped run my family's household under similar circumstances back in California, but life in England was different: it felt like we had been blasted back into Dickens's time. The automatic washing machines we had back home weren't yet commonplace in the U.K., so I had to do laundry by hand: first, boil the clothes in a copper boiler, then run the load through the wringer, rinse, wring again, then hang it all out to dry. By the time I had finished one load, I felt more than justified in rewarding myself with a trip to town to indulge in books and cats.

I frequented the county library, which was presided over by a resident cat, and I'd pop into the bookstore nearby, which also had a full-time feline who spent most of the day snoozing on a big cart of books parked out in front of the store. We couldn't buy a lot of books because we didn't have much money, but the shopkeeper didn't mind if I stood there all day long reading a book, as long as I didn't walk off with it. Then I'd grab a cup of tea to visit with yet another cat at one of the cafés in town before I headed home.

You wouldn't think there'd be a mouse left in England with all those cats, but many farms had gone fallow after the war—family members had either died during the war or moved away—and the rodents had taken over the fields.

We even got a cat of our own on a trip south to Cornwall, in a town appropriately named Mousehole. We were petting one of the cats down at the docks when one of the fishermen approached us.

"His name's Fred."

I looked at the cat, a black-and-white tuxedo cat. "Fred's a good name."

"Would you like him?"

"Why? He doesn't like fish?"

"He likes the food at the pub better," he said, sticking a thumb in the pub's general direction. "He keeps stealing the food."

I looked at my husband. We both missed having a cat of our own. He shrugged. "Sure."

"Then that's settled," the fisherman said. "He's yours."

We put him in a box and drove him back to Conington. He sat the whole time without making a sound. Once in a while, I'd lift the lid and reach in to scratch his head and he purred.

Books and cats again. What more could I want?

We ended up sharing Fred with our landlord, who served as the librarian at Cambridge University, and who let me read from his complete collection of Dickens and Thackeray, which I devoured. When it came time to head back to the States after two years, I was sad to leave, but we found Fred a new home in

East Anglia where he had his own room and lived a long and happy life.

⚬

A freshly minted professor's teaching salary only goes so far, so I had to go to work. We were back in California living in Ventura County, and since I had no degree, the pool of available jobs was limited.

I took the first job that was offered to me, as a technician at Camarillo State Hospital, one of the largest mental hospitals in the country at the time, and where the notorious movie *The Snake Pit* was filmed.

I thought I'd be helping out with patients, but one of my first assignments was to find and kill flies and put them on a sheet of typing paper. It wasn't difficult, since Camarillo was a farming community and flies were in great abundance. At our monthly staff meeting, the head of psychiatric services demanded that the nursing staff arrange eight dead flies—no more, no less—on a sheet of typing paper in front of his place at the head of the table to show that we were alert to the contagion and the annoyance of flies.

I went on a fly-killing safari and kept my mouth shut. The hospital was straight out of *One Flew Over the Cuckoo's Nest* and I hated my job, but I couldn't leave. Given my lack of experience and credentials, jobs were few and far between.

After my shift, I'd come home and dive into whatever book I was reading that day. I couldn't make it through five books in a day—let alone ten—but I was still a fast reader. And books were a great way to escape.

Once we returned to the States, I knew we'd be moving often so my husband could build up his teaching and research résumé. I didn't think it was fair to keep pets when we'd be moving around for the foreseeable future, so I doubled down on my book habit to compensate. As it turned out, we'd end up changing residences so often that we didn't open some of our wedding presents until we'd been married ten years.

In 1956, we moved to Oberlin, Ohio, where I became pregnant with my daughter Julia two years later. My labor went on for hours and I needed something to read between contractions, so the hospital volunteer who ran the library cart and I were on pretty friendly terms by the time I finally gave birth. And when my son Martin was born in Syracuse, New York, in 1962, I managed to make it through a couple of mysteries by the time he showed up.

In 1964, my husband accepted a job at Claremont Graduate School in California, and we finally settled down. *Now* we could get animals. Little did I know that we'd moved into the perfect neighborhood for animal lovers.

One set of neighbors ran a pet shop, and they frequently brought some of their "merchandise" home. They had a chimpanzee who'd regularly break out and cruise the neighborhood. When he banged on our door—which happened with some frequency—Julia would give him a cookie, take his hand, and walk him back home.

The woman who lived behind us kept a swimming pool full of huge tortoises, and one day she decided to give us one. We named him Greased Lightning and he more than lived up to his name by running away from home at least once a week. We also had an opossum living in the eucalyptus tree in our yard.

Julia had inherited my animal-loving genes, and it didn't

take long before she started her own one-girl rescue operation. One day I noticed a funny smell coming from her room but I couldn't pinpoint the source. I started to put her clean laundry away, and when I opened her underwear drawer I came face-to-face with a boa constrictor. I quickly shut the drawer—I loved animals but drew the line at snakes—and checked for other living things, quick *and* slow moving. I opened her closet and saw a small cage pushed into the back behind her shoes.

A rat, aka the boa's dinner.

Apparently the pet shop owner had been regularly giving her merchandise as a reward for returning the chimp, but I made her take both snake and rat back to the shop.

———◦•◦———

I was thrilled to not have to pack up and move anymore. And I loved being a mother.

But I felt something shift in my marriage. My husband started to withdraw from me and the kids. It was nothing major at first, but it was enough so that we all noticed. The kids got clingier first with him, and then with me.

In 1969, my husband was an established professor who was well-known in his field, and he told me that his workload required him to spend more time away from home in meetings and traveling. I rarely questioned it. After all, how would I know how much time he needed to meet with students or go over their term papers? We all had our responsibilities and sacrifices to make, and this was part of being a wife and mother.

But I did think it was strange that we never had very much money. One day, everything suddenly made sense when he sat me down and told me point-blank that our marriage was no longer working and that he wanted a divorce.

You know the feeling when you suddenly leave your body and seem to be looking over your shoulder at a scene that feels real and surreal at the same time?

That's how it felt when he uttered that one simple sentence.

I stared at him, then I started to laugh. At that point, we'd been married for almost twenty years.

"Okay, so what's the joke?"

"It's not a joke."

I stood up, too calmly, I thought, again watching myself from the remove of some dreamlike distance. But my mind went wild as I made a checklist of everything I needed to do.

For me, it was absolutely over, and at that moment, as I saw it, I had only two choices.

I could stay in California to raise my kids while working at the only minimum-wage low-skill jobs that were open to me. But I knew it wouldn't be enough for even a cheap apartment. Besides, a college community can be very close-knit, where everybody knows everyone's business and then some. I didn't want to subject myself or my kids to that kind of environment.

Or I could move. My parents had recently bought a small ranch in a tiny town called Genoa, Nevada, in the foothills of the Sierra Nevadas, and the kids and I spent a few weeks there every summer, riding horses, hiking, and visiting.

My family was still fiercely close. They'd take me in and help support me and the kids while I got my feet back on the ground.

As I saw it, I didn't have much choice.

EIGHT

<hr/>

When something needs to get done, I morph into Super-woman, transforming into a model of cold, clear-eyed efficiency. Once I decided to leave my marriage, I shipped the kids off to my parents and started to pack up my life. I was detached yet methodical, and got everything done as fast as I could.

Indeed, three months later, I'd moved my kids, myself, and my things to Genoa and was granted a divorce in Carson City. I've never seen anything so quick as that divorce; the judge talked so fast I couldn't understand a word he said.

But it was over. Well, not really; in a way, I knew that everything was just starting.

<hr/>

My parents were livid. They were thoroughly old-school: you married for life and you supported your family through hell or high water.

True to her Italian revenge-based ancestry, my mother decided to do something about it. She baked a cake, packed it up, and dropped it off at the post office addressed to my ex-husband. When my father asked why she was sending her former son-in-law a cake, she smiled cryptically, mentioning something about a secret ingredient.

My father frowned. He well knew her family's volatile Italian history. "*What* secret ingredient?"

"A pinch of arsenic."

My father flew out of the house and down to the post office and convinced the postmaster to give him back the package even though it was against federal regulations. Dad promised he wouldn't tell anyone or else the postmaster would lose his job.

Even though my parents helped me immeasurably, I still had to adjust to life as a single mother. I had very little money, two kids, and was living off my parents. I received a hundred dollars a month in child support for each of the kids and the princely sum of one dollar a year in alimony. I could have fought for more, but honestly, I just wanted everything to be over with so I could get on with my life.

I had to learn how to manage my meager finances and pay the bills, but on the bright side it was kind of refreshing because at least now I knew exactly where the money was going.

Fortunately, the kids adjusted relatively quickly. After all, they were already familiar with life on a ranch. Plus, it was easy to meet people in town because my father already knew most of them, so we were accepted into the community as part of his family.

As divorced parents everywhere know, I had to try to stay upbeat for the children, rolling out the old standard spiel:

"Your daddy loves you, your mommy loves you, but they're not getting along anymore so it's better if we don't live in the same house." I didn't want my children to be burdened by the breakup—Julia was eleven and Martin was seven—so I had to stay as positive as I could manage for the first few months after the divorce until I knew they were okay.

I was exhausted but I held it together while I went through the process of moving on from a twenty-year relationship. It wasn't easy.

———

At first, it felt like I was living inside a room where all the windows were covered in Vaseline: blurry and unfathomable. I knew there was a world outside where all sorts of wonderful things were going on, but I lacked the energy and desire to pursue any of them.

My parents—and the animals—did their best to try to cheer me up. My father had graduated from the small mixed breeds and terriers of my childhood to larger dogs like German shepherds and Labradors. His favorite Lab was a stellar hunting dog who was not the least gun-shy, but who instead cowered in fear in the presence of a tiny duckling, deathly afraid of the very creature he was supposed to excel at pursuing.

It was comical, but it was hard for me to laugh at anything. I just couldn't get past the betrayal. My mother had a special radar for my moods, and when I got really mopey, she'd step in and put me to work.

"Go pick up the mail, please," she said one day. "And take Pan with you." Pan was a Nubian goat who liked to go for walks through the town. He even had his own leash.

The post office was only a few blocks away, and off we went. Instead of tying him up outside, I brought him into the tiny office, and in the few seconds it took to fetch the mail from the box, Pan had already chewed through a couple of the Wanted posters that hung on the wall.

"Pan!" I admonished him, quickly leading him outside. "Bad goat!"

The goat was startled, but so was I. His antics had broken through my fog—at least for a few seconds—but as we headed home my thoughts returned to why I was taking a goat on a walk to the post office in a tiny town in Nevada—and not in California—and the fog descended once more.

My mother told me to pick up the mail again the next day, and the next, and so on. My fog lifted for a minute or two longer each day and it got a little easier. I started to look forward to watching Pan chow down on the posters, which I noticed were replaced every few days. He had taken a particular liking to the poster of Angela Davis, a political radical and head of the Communist Party in the U.S., but after a few weeks the postmaster caught on and one day there were no more posters, though Davis was still at large.

Besides the animals, of course my beloved books also helped. They let me escape, even for an hour or two, and forget everything. Little by little, I started to feel better each day, and decided it was time for me to get on with life. I felt obligated to take some of the financial burden off my parents while also helping to pitch in with chores around the ranch. After all, they were well into their sixties by then.

I started to look for a job but I knew it wouldn't be easy. Employment prospects around the Carson Valley were not plentiful—they still aren't today—and back then, most jobs were agricultural in nature. My meager experience in health care and libraries wouldn't be of much help.

Besides, I was living in a very different kind of place from what I was used to. To say I was experiencing a bit of a culture shock was an understatement. After all, I had moved from a college town with a population of twenty-four thousand in one of the most densely populated counties in the country to a rough-and-tumble town in the dusty foothills of the Sierra Nevadas. The population of Genoa was a whopping 137 when I landed there in the summer of 1969. Actually, just by virtue of the three of us moving there we caused the population to spike by almost three percent.

Genoa was best-known for being the first settled town in Nevada and for town meetings that would erupt in violence more often than not. Coming as I did from the genteel world of academics and professors, it was a bit of a jolt.

Today, Highway 395 is a busy four-lane highway with a speed limit of seventy. But back then it wasn't unusual to see a dog or two lying out in the middle of the road; drivers would know enough to slow down and go around them. There were two markets in town, and after I'd been in a couple of times the cashiers greeted me by name and opened a store account for me. When I brought my kids up to the meat counter, the butcher would hand them a hot dog instead of a lollipop.

It was that kind of place.

So was the county library in Minden, the county seat, a postage-stamp-sized building that nevertheless was crammed to the gills with books of every stripe, though the quantity and selection was a fraction of the size of those in libraries I'd frequented back in California.

I signed up for a library card and promptly dove into the Mystery section. I picked out an armful—though not in alphabetical order—and brought them up to the counter where the librarian on duty stamped them.

"Mysteries, huh?" she said. "I love them too, can't get enough." She paused, then looked me in the eye. "I always identify with the murderer."

I nodded. "They help me get rid of all my aggressions."

"That, too," she replied and held out her hand. "Yvonne Saddler."

"Jan Louch." I shook her hand. "Pleased to meet you."

We chatted about a few authors we both liked, and she gave me a heads-up on a few new mysteries she thought I might like.

From that day forward, whenever I returned books and checked out new ones, Yvonne and I would compare notes and chat about the various comings and goings in town.

Every time I walked in the door, I thought back to how much I had loved working in a library. But the Douglas County Library was so small—I'd noticed only one other employee—I was sure that jobs rarely opened up and that there was already a long line of people who would get first dibs.

I doubled down on my job hunting but nothing materialized. One day my mother told me that she knew a man who was looking for someone who could handle his correspondence and secretarial work and who also needed some help getting around because he had only one leg and was getting on in years.

My nursing experience at Camarillo and typing up endless papers for my ex got me the job.

After a year or so, the man needed more care than I could provide, so I had to find another job. I heard that a restaurant in Genoa called the Pink House was looking for a fine European chef. I knew how to cook meals for the kids, of course, and figured my rudimentary skills were transferable up to a point, so I headed over and applied for the job.

"Why, yes, I'm a chef," I said, and they told me to come back the next day for a trial run. I followed the recipes they gave me, and though the dishes bore no resemblance to the meat loaf and spaghetti I typically prepared at home, it worked. I started the next day.

To commute to work, I rode one of my parents' horses named Angel and hitched her up right in front of the restaurant. After my shift, I tied a flashlight to her tail so drivers could see us in the dark and headed back to the ranch.

I left the restaurant after a year or so and I found a job with the local agricultural extension service, which helps local farmers and ranches improve their businesses. In particular, I was hired to help children in 4-H learn to raise their sheep and cows and prepare them for competition. What did I know about livestock? Not much, but I'd picked up a few things from living on a twenty-acre ranchette with my parents, though they treated all of their animals like pets, not as potential meals. After five years I moved on to a job with the local chamber of commerce where I visited businesses, replaced brochures in racks, and attended more local government meetings than anyone should be subjected to over five lifetimes.

Since I'd moved to Genoa, I had begun to feel better, made

some friends, and even went out on dates. But I still felt beaten down by my divorce. One day I was cooking dinner for the family when I noticed my mother staring at me.

"What?"

"Why don't you laugh anymore?" she asked.

"I laugh."

She shook her head. "Not like you used to."

I grunted something back at her, but I knew she was right. Despite growing up during a pretty grim time, one thing our family did was laugh. *A lot.* Though our humor often bordered on sarcasm and we could occasionally be really gross and abusive to one another, it was what we knew and how we related. And we always understood that it was done with great love and affection.

I wanted to move on with my life but I felt stuck, though I was doing my best to raise my family in a seemingly normal way: helping my kids with their homework, and handling the bulk of the cooking. My mother hated to cook and used to burn pots on the stove at least once a week; her forte was gardening and painting, and she'd much rather be spending her time on these pursuits. One day, she tried to parboil eggs in a pressure cooker and blew the lid off so the eggs shot right up to the ceiling and were stuck there for days. Another time, she decided to make some bread and went way overboard on the yeast. She put it in the oven to rise, and it rose so much that it pushed the door open. We put it out for the animals, but they wouldn't touch it.

The Carson Valley was a great place to live with my family and call home. But I wanted to feel at home with my job. I was grateful for the jobs I'd had since I moved to Genoa, but I wanted to do something that I loved and also where politics was not a blood sport.

One day, I went into the library to return some books and Yvonne pulled me aside.

A staff member was retiring, she said, and asked if I was interested in the job.

I said, *Oh God, of course. How much do I pay you?*

Not really. But I filled out an application and tried to temper my hopes of ever being hired for the position.

***

But I *was* hired. And I was in heaven.

However, I quickly found out that the life of a librarian is frequently misunderstood.

In popular culture, the biggest misconception about librarians is that we run around hissing "shush" to anyone within shouting distance, and that we're rigid and on the stuffy side.

Not true. Many librarians I've met through the years have secret lives that are wild and filled with abandon. We are very serious about the work, but after work, anything goes. While I take great issue with the word "rigid," I will admit that librarians care very deeply about keeping everything right where it's supposed to be, otherwise how is anyone going to find the book they're looking for? Bent instead of being rigid, we are flexible in our jobs, almost to a fault. You almost have to be when you're dealing with so many different kinds of people walking through the door every single day.

I'd be the first to admit that my own misconceptions about the job were blown out of the water in my first few days working at the Douglas County Library as assistant county librarian in charge of reference. I thought I'd spend my days happily recommending books to patrons, thumbing through thick reference books to answer their questions, and stamping books.

Oh, how wrong I was. I hit the ground running my first day. After all, there were only two full-time employees—Yvonne and me—one part-time worker, and a handful of elderly volunteers who usually needed us to help them shelve the books.

It didn't take long to discover how much work being a librarian actually is. Most people think, oh, all you do is check out books, but they don't realize what has to happen before a book ever reaches their hands: first we select and order the book, then once it arrives we have to cover the book and enter it into the catalog or database. Then, sometimes only a short time later if the book is popular, we often have to repair the book. Finally, if it's no longer valid as an information source we need to remove it from the shelves and either discard it or give it to the Friends of the Library who can hopefully sell it and raise a buck or two. Then we have to research and purchase another book to replace it.

Since Yvonne was busy with the administrative side of running the library and dealing with county commissioners, I was the one whom patrons approached when they couldn't find the answer to a question, whether for a school paper or out of idle curiosity.

The first couple of times that somebody asked a question, I was somewhat stunned that I was getting paid to do something that I loved to do. For me, it killed two birds with one stone: I learned something new, plus I was able to help a patron. When it comes right down to it, I think that for every librarian, on some level the most important part of the job is helping people. Through the years, this has played out time and again as I've watched those who took the job for other reasons rarely last more than a few months before quitting.

Librarians may not know everything, but we certainly know where to look for it. I love finding little tidbits of knowledge that I didn't know before. In a way, I've always felt a little like Columbus: wow, I've discovered something new.

Sometimes it took only a few seconds to find the answer, for example, *How do you spell "Peloponnesus"?* Other times, my quest dragged on for months. Today, of course, anyone can look up pretty much anything online and an answer will pop up, correct or not. But when we were just dealing with hard copy—books, journals, newspapers, microfiche, and the like—it was more difficult because our reference collection was pretty limited. If I couldn't find the answer in our own collection, I'd have to turn to other libraries around the state through interlibrary loan, which took a bit of finesse to master. And a lot of detective work.

I came up against dead ends all the time. After all, databases are not kept up-to-date, a book may have been lost or stolen—or it grew legs, as we sometimes said—or it might currently be checked out or was reference only. But I kept going. There were only a handful of times in my entire career that I couldn't find the answer to a patron's question. I think I felt worse than the patron, who, more often than not, had completely forgotten about the request in the interim.

Another thing is that librarians don't like to say no to people. I hated to tell a patron that I couldn't help or find what he was looking for, because I viewed it as a personal failure.

At other times, people didn't like the answer I found. For example, once a patron asked me to research how many cows were rustled on a particular ranch in 1872; she thought it was twenty-five cows but she wanted to be sure. Luckily, I knew we already had the book with the answer in our own collection of historical documents about Nevada. I flipped to the property report, which listed only three cows rustled that year.

She frowned. "You're wrong."

I turned the book around so she could see. "That's what it says," I said. "You do know that in the 1870s three cows was a year's income?"

"It's still wrong," she huffed, and stomped out.

I closed the book. I was slightly flustered; after all, my research skills had been called into question. But then I realized that even though it was there in black-and-white, the woman had probably built up the history of the ranch in her mind for years: she envisioned it as a huge, sprawling ranch with an enormous number of cows and seventeen cowboys rustling them around all day *yippy-ki-yaying* and stuff. And I had committed the great sin of reducing it to a subsistence-level family ranch.

Happily, most people were thrilled that I could answer their questions at all, regardless of the outcome. One day, Joyce Hollister, the *Record-Courier* reporter and also a friend, came in to check where a particular quote came from.

"Those who don't learn from history are condemned to repeat it."

I pulled out *Bartlett's Familiar Quotations* and flipped to the back. To use the book, you look up a particular word or phrase from the quote, which then cross-references quotes that also list the author and source. I feverishly flipped through the pages as dust particles launched into the air. Joyce sneezed, but I didn't; after all, I was accustomed to the dust that lived in these massive books.

For Joyce's question, I used the word "history," but her quote wasn't listed. However, instead of admitting defeat, I reacted as if the book had thrown down the gauntlet. I knew the answer was in there somewhere.

"Forget it," she said. "It's not important."

I didn't hear her. I was like a dog with a bone. I *had* to find the answer, or it would bug me for the rest of the night. No, to be completely honest, it would torture me for the rest of my life unless I located the source.

I frowned and looked at the quote again. Something wasn't quite right.

"Maybe it's not 'history' but some other word," I said.

"No, really, it's okay," Joyce repeated.

I ignored her and flipped through a few more pages to try out a few more words. What about 'past'?

And then, just like magic, there was the quote. One word had made all the difference.

" 'Those who don't remember the *past* are condemned to repeat it,' " I said, smiling. "George Santayana originally said it." I put the quotation book away and pulled out another book, a biographical resource about famous people throughout history. "He was a Spanish-American philosopher who . . ."

"Thank you," said Joyce, who turned around and left. She probably had a deadline to meet.

But I continued to read about Santayana. *Happily.*

———◦◦◦———

Even though I enjoyed helping people, it didn't mean I did so with a smile twenty-four/seven. After all, it's never been my nature to walk around grinning all day. That, coupled with the stress of learning a new job—no matter how much I loved it—as well as the lingering inability to move beyond my busted-up marriage, gave me a reputation for being gruff around the library. And while I shuddered to think anyone could confuse me with the diabolical librarian of my childhood who restricted me to a mere five books a day, I told myself that my being in charge of collecting overdue book fines from patrons was a big part of my rep.

Ten years had passed since I moved to the Carson Valley. Some days were still difficult, but I had made a life for myself. I had my family, a few good friends, a boatload of animals, and my dream job.

I still couldn't believe that I was getting paid to work around books and learn new things every day.

Little did I know it was about to get much, much better with the addition of two furry employees.

LIBRARY CAT PROFILE: ELSIE

Elsie is a jet-black cat who moved into the St. Helena Public Library in St. Helena, California, in the spring of 2012. She wears a tag hanging from her collar that says "Elsie the library cat" on one side, and "I'm not supposed to check out" on the other. She was named for Elsie Wood, a major donor to the library. She has her own Facebook page: Elsie the Library Cat.

1) *How did you end up living at the library?*

I was adopted from a local shelter for the specific purpose of becoming a library cat. The library had a mouse problem and the library staff—who had been looking for an excuse to get a cat—decided to pounce on the opportunity. By the way, I've never caught a mouse, nor do I intend to. Mice are gross. But the library brought in a human pest specialist who took care of that problem.

2) *What are some of your jobs at the library?*

I greet staff every morning and update them on all goings-on of the previous night. I also help to investigate file drawers, unpack boxes, and generally manage by walking around. Since I am the only staff member who can fit, I am also responsible for checking the attic crawl spaces as needed. I always sit on the best books, so if you are looking for a good read, check underneath me. And speaking of sitting, one of my most important tasks is keeping the cushion at the front desk from floating away. This assignment takes up a lot of my time so I often multitask with either a bath or nap.

3) *What are some of your pet peeves about your job?*

I hate closed doors. I feel that they hamper my ability to do my job thoroughly. I cannot adequately patrol and supervise if I am kept out of areas that require attention. I also don't like being picked up. Some patrons who are self-proclaimed "cat people" will insist on picking me up and I do not like it. For the same reason, I don't like closing time since it usually means I will be picked up and taken to the staff area for the night, which also means a closed door.

4) *Who are some of your favorite patrons, and why?*

I know it's not very politically correct, but my favorite people are smokers. I don't know why but I just love the smell of cigarettes and will immediately make friends with anyone who smokes them. I also like to roll around on books and DVDs that are returned by smokers. I also tend to like people who are shy and quiet and don't have very good social skills. They seem to like me too since I don't judge them.

5) *What is your favorite book?*

Apart from books that smell like cigarette smoke, I like *I Could Pee on This* and *Sid the Six-Dinner Cat.*

6) *Do you have advice for other library cats?*

Find the most resonant parts of the building to practice your singing. Make your demands known early and often. Practice hiding in plain sight at closing time. The staff finds this game very entertaining, so much so that they will stay late just to play it. Chase is also a fun closing-time game. A word of caution though, don't do it too frequently or you may find yourself being "taken to the back" earlier in the evening. Don't sit on laps unless you are invited. And never, ever sit under the book chute.

7) *Do you have any advice for librarians who'd like to add a cat to their staff?*

Get a rescue kitty, preferably a black one and a "mature" cat. We tend to be more mellow and are hardest for shelters to find homes for. I lived at the shelter for several months before the library adopted me. Put air filters in the children's room or any enclosed spaces that aren't well ventilated. It helps cut down on the whole allergy thing. [Actually, in more than three years the library has never had a single complaint about me causing allergic reactions, but this is a good "insurance" message.] Make sure your kitty is microchipped, and if you think your kitty might go outside, consider a GPS collar. Having a library cat gives you a great opportunity to be an ambassador for your local shelter. My library has collected food donations and other items for the shelter and also helps find homes for emergency cases.

8) *Anything else you'd like to add?*

Like me on Facebook!

NINE

―◦•◦―

Nineteen eighty-five marked a milestone for the town of Minden.

That was the year we got our first traffic light, at the corner of Routes 395 and 88.

Both newcomers and natives lamented what that symbolized, though some did manage to view it as a sign of progress. Genoa, just to the north, was still tiny, but new subdivisions of forty and fifty houses were being developed throughout the valley.

In addition to the new library in Minden, the county also had a small branch library up at Zephyr Cove on the east side of Lake Tahoe, and some of the staff at the Minden branch occasionally worked at this much smaller library, which meant driving twenty miles on switchbacks up the Sierra Nevada range, with a corresponding two-thousand-foot rise in altitude. Some staffers didn't like the drive since it could be especially harrowing in winter—and at any time for those afraid of heights—but the view it provided across the valley was stunning.

It was also the best way to see how fast the area was growing. I liked to pull off into one of the rest areas and look across to the Pine Nut Mountains on the other side of the valley. In the 1970s, you'd mostly see cattle grazing. Now there were a lot fewer cattle in the daytime, and at night there were a lot more lights. And they used to be separated; you'd see a pocket of lights dotting the landscape and recognize the separate towns and villages as Minden and Gardnerville.

Now they were starting to blur together.

So many people were moving to the Carson Valley that we were quickly losing the intimacy that came from living in a place where everyone knew everybody else. Besides the traffic light, a simple trip to the grocery store was the best way to measure this: I'd still stop and chat with people, but I was starting to see people who didn't have a clue who I was and vice versa. They were just people out shopping.

The whole dynamic of the community was starting to change.

———◆·◆———

Our arrangement with Baker & Taylor had gone smoothly so far. Bill told us that librarians were flocking to their booths at regional and national conventions, clamoring for a poster or two of their own. After they returned home, they'd hang up the poster at their library, which started a chain reaction: if they put it in the workroom, the staff would stare at the poster for a good chunk of the day and soon want one of their own.

Other librarians wanted to share the cats with their patrons, and they'd hang their posters in their main reading room or above the circulation desk, which is what we did. Sometimes patrons would get a little confused. They'd look at the poster, then at the cats, and then back at the poster. Finally, they'd ask, "How did you get two cats that look just like the ones on the poster?"

Hanging the poster where patrons could see it usually set off a whole new flurry of requests for posters. The line that ran along the lower edge of the first poster read: "Feline Literati Society, Douglas County Library, Minden, Nevada," so it wasn't unusual for envelopes to be addressed to the "Feline Literati Society."

People would also write or call the Baker & Taylor company directly, and librarians would ask their sales rep for a copy. Bill provided us with a steady supply, but our stash would run low on a regular basis. We didn't charge for the posters—and neither did Baker & Taylor—though people would occasionally enclose a dollar or two to cover the shipping costs, which we stuffed into the petty cash jar that I'd dip into whenever I needed to buy cat food or kitty litter.

We didn't think twice about spending money on the cats of course, and we didn't scrimp on them, either; we loved to share the cats with the world and make people happy. But it was costing us money, and we vowed from the start not to use a penny of taxpayer money.

Our budgets were tight, and Yvonne and I were covering all of the cats' expenses—from cat food and kitty litter to regular vet checkups—out of our own pockets, and most weeks there was little money left over. When Bill stopped by to discuss another photo shoot we mentioned our financial situation to him, and he promised that he would handle it. The company drew up a formal contract for the exclusive right to use Baker and Taylor in their advertising and promotional campaigns and would pay us a set fee to cover our feline expenses.

A week later, Yvonne and I signed the agreement on the cats' behalf, and we had a check for $2,500 soon afterward. We breathed a sigh of relief. Yvonne and I split the money to cover what we'd shelled out for food, litter, toys, and vet bills in the two years since the cats arrived.

Today, with YouTube, Twitter, Facebook, and six-figure endorsement deals for celebrity cats from Grumpy Cat to Maru, this kind of arrangement would be laughable. But for us, it wasn't about the money, rather the fact that Baker and Taylor were making people all over the country feel good about books and reading.

The next photo shoot would take place the following month.

⊸•⊷

As before, we scheduled the photo shoot for a Sunday.

This time, Baker & Taylor had a definite idea about the kinds of photos they wanted for different markets. In addition to Bill, a couple of other people from Baker & Taylor showed up to give specific instructions about how they wanted the cats to pose.

They also brought lots of props, unlike the last time when we had to raid the cats' own toy stash. A couple of stylists and photo assistants bustled around and brought out a lunch box for ads aimed at school librarians and an old-fashioned cash register for bookstores. The company also wanted to get some pictures of the cats with books, "the older the better," we were instructed.

I knew just the thing: an old leather-bound dictionary that dated back to the early twentieth century. It sat on a podium stand in the reference room.

Whether they wanted to put the cats on top of the book—which I wasn't crazy about since they'd probably dig their claws right in and damage the book—or next to it, I had no idea, but I wheeled it out into the library.

When the photographer was finished setting up, I let the cats out of the workroom. They were instantly wary, and took slow tentative steps toward us. After all, they'd seen the lights and cameras before. They knew it wasn't a pleasant experience.

It turned out to be a lot more work for us than on the previous shoot. We posed them as the photographer and executives called out directions to us: have them sit together looking at each other. Now make them face in the opposite direction. Now stand them up. How about lying down?

The photographer and executives were very businesslike. They came in and said we need this, and this, and this, and this, and the cats just metaphorically stuck their tongues out at them saying, *You'll get what we give and that's it.* Baker and Taylor were absolutely wonderful animals except when someone wanted to make them do something they didn't want to do.

They particularly hated having to pose in one position and then move into another, especially when it wasn't a position that they actually wanted to be in. So they kept trying to run away, but we kept petting them and saying it was all right, and glared at the photographer like they did. And just like the last time, we stood behind the photographer making chirpy noises and dangling toys and tossing over the occasional kitty treat to get them to comply.

The photographer worked as fast as he could, but finally they'd just had it and refused to pose anymore.

I couldn't blame them; I don't like being forced into unnatural positions, either.

We broke for lunch, and for once I didn't have to herd the cats into the workroom; they wanted to be as far away from the backdrop, props, and flashing lights as possible.

"Time for the dictionary," the photographer announced after we regrouped.

The dictionary was open on a stand that swiveled from side to side, so Yvonne and I braced it in order to keep it steady.

"Can you pose the cats so their paws are draped over the book and we only see them from the shoulders up?" the photographer asked as he swapped out lenses.

All of the chairs in the library were standard height; plus it would take several boxes stacked up to reach the dictionary stand. "We don't have anything high enough for them to sit on," I said.

"Then can you just hold them?"

I sighed. It wasn't going to be easy. After all, these were not cats who liked to be held. I looked at Baker and Taylor on the floor, distracted by their treats and full stomachs. I apologized to them in advance for what Yvonne and I were about to do to them. I knew the only way to make it up to them was with copious amounts of cantaloupe and yogurt when it was all over.

"We'll do our best," I replied.

I waited until the photographer was ready, then took a deep

When I was two years old, animals and I were already inseparable. Here I am with our dog Snowy. *Courtesy Jan Louch*

Pan was my parents' Nubian goat who loved to walk on a leash and dine on old vegetables out of the refrigerator's crisper drawer. *Courtesy Jan Louch*

Like most cats, Baker could never resist a box, especially if it had his name on it. *Courtesy Jan Louch*

Baker liked an engaging game of checkers, though if someone lost interest, he'd sprawl across the board, thus ending the game. *Courtesy Jan Louch*

In his younger days, Baker liked to supervise from on high. *Courtesy Jan Louch*

Many Scottish Folds like to sit in an upright position, but Taylor had elevated it to an art form, like this . . . *Courtesy Jan Louch*

. . . and this. *Courtesy Jan Louch*

It wasn't unusual for Taylor to lick a yogurt container completely clean, but sometimes he got his head stuck and we had to come to his rescue. *Courtesy Jan Louch*

Both cats loved the Christmas season because of all the shiny things . . . and the leftover holiday turkey. *Courtesy Jan Louch*

INFORMATION NEVADA INTERLIBRARY LOAN **SUBJECT** REQUEST

Date of request: April 10, 1984

Via:

Send green and yellow copies, retain gold copy.

Requesting library:
North Las Vegas Library
2300 Civic Center Dr.
North Las Vegas, NV 89030

To be used for (be specific):
☐ Business or professional
☐ General interest
☐ Research
☐ School
☐ Other Pleasure

☐ URGENT (do not reserve)
☐ Needed by
☐ General interest (Nev. only)
☐ Serious interest (Nev./Calif.)
☐ Must have (wherever possible)
Priority:

Patron:
Address:
Linda Stapley
Staff

Tel.:

SUBJECT REQUEST: (please describe in detail exactly what patron wants and for what purpose.)

1 Scottish Fold kitty - male or female

PLEASE DO NOT MAIL IN BOOK BAG

We have already provided: none in North Las Vegas

Level of knowledge (expert or beginner):

Amount of information needed (books only, articles OK, etc.):

Will pay up to $ _____ for photocopy.
Suggested titles if any:

Request taken by:

FOR LENDING LIBRARY · Sending: (Briefly. Books require separate forms.)

Douglas County Library

From:
☐ BIP Sub
☐ LC Bks Sub
☐ CCLD Cat
☐ RG
☑ Other Poster

We have checked:
☐ RG
☑ Mon Cat
☐ Other

Patrons often asked if they could check out one—or both—of the cats, but one librarian made her interlibrary loan request in the usual way. *Courtesy Jan Louch*

BAKER AND TAYLOR: TWO LIBRARY CATS

The cats' first poster, which launched their worldwide fame. *Courtesy Baker & Taylor, LLC*

Baker's job title was Official Greeter, though he fell asleep on the job more often than not . . .
Courtesy Jan Louch

. . . over and . . .
Courtesy Jan Louch

. . . over and . . .
Courtesy Jan Louch

. . . over again.
Courtesy Jan Louch

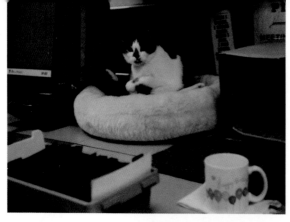

Taylor's favorite spot was at my desk with his Happy Birthday mug within paw's reach.
Courtesy Jan Louch

Like Baker, Taylor also appreciated a good box.
Courtesy Jan Louch

Common stress spots—those most affected by too much anxiety—include the bladder, fur, skin, and the anal glands located at the base of the tail.

Special Mention
TAYLOR BOOKS—Mascot of the Minden, Nevada, Library.

THURSDAY
DECEMBER
1994
29

Taylor once graced the pages of the 365 Cats Page-A-Day Calendar.

The poster that resulted from the cats' second photo shoot made the cats even more well-known. *Courtesy Baker & Taylor, LLC*

In addition to posters, Baker & Taylor also created a series of ads based on famous works of art that also featured the cats. *Courtesy Baker & Taylor, LLC*

The second photo shoot with the cats featured a variety of props that would result in ads to appeal to specific audiences, like school librarians in this instance. *Courtesy Baker & Taylor, LLC*

The cats took turns sitting on top of our computers back in the day when the nice toasty monitors were the size of a microwave oven. *Courtesy Baker & Taylor, LLC*

Though the cats had very different personalities, they were rarely separated throughout their lives. *Courtesy Baker & Taylor, LLC*

Patrons soon grew accustomed to seeing a couple of cats with funny ears just hanging out around the library. *Courtesy Jan Louch*

The cats never knew they were famous; they only knew there were a lot of people willing to entertain them. *Courtesy Jan Louch*

The circulation desk was where Baker spent the majority of his time when the library was open. *Courtesy Jan Louch*

Baker's second favorite spot was sprawled on his back near the front door, where he made it almost impossible to not rub his belly as patrons entered. *Courtesy Jan Louch*

He sometimes helped out with checking out books, where our productivity was sometimes less than optimal given all the head pats and scratches that were involved. *Courtesy Jan Louch*

Happy Holidays…

In addition to using the cats in ads, posters, and promotional items, the Baker & Taylor company also used them in their holiday correspondence. *Courtesy Baker & Taylor, LLC*

Neither cat liked to be held, but they indulged me every so often even when someone was wielding a much-hated camera. *Courtesy Jan Louch*

The human-sized Baker and Taylor costumes are still used at library and bookseller trade shows and conventions today. *Courtesy Jan Louch*

In 1989 when this ad appeared, the cats were the cornerstone of Baker & Taylor's advertising campaigns. *Courtesy Baker & Taylor, LLC*

Leslie Kramm launched the Baker and Taylor Fan Club in 1990 to help her second-graders with their studies. *Courtesy Leslie Kramm Twigg*

Members of the fan club wearing their hand-colored Baker and Taylor masks. *Courtesy Leslie Kramm Twigg*

Leslie Kramm devoted an entire wall of her classroom to photos, posters, and drawings of the cats. *Courtesy Leslie Kramm Twigg*

Whenever the fan club sent us their drawings, we hung them up on the wall in the children's section. Here, Baker shows his approval. *Courtesy Jan Louch*

When Baker died in 1994, all the staff members signed a notecard from Baker & Taylor Books to send to anyone who had sent a sympathy card or donated a book to the library. I added the angel wings and halo on Baker along with a puddle of tears surrounding Taylor. *Courtesy Jan Louch*

Patron Joseph Figini loved books and cats, and he was a frequent visitor at the library. *Courtesy Claudia Bertolone-Smith*

douglas county public library

December 19, 1997

Dear Baker and Taylor Fan Club,

I was so happy to receive your letters. We put them up in the children's room at the library where I live. Some of you asked me how old I am. I am 15. In cat years I am 105 years old!! That is pretty old for a cat. I am not feeling very well. I have cancer. Today has been a bad day and Jan is going to come get me and take me to the vet. He will put me to sleep so I won't hurt anymore.

I feel sad about dying because I will miss your letters. I always look forward to receiving your letters and the great cat books Ms. Kramm has sent to our library with all your names in them. We put your Christmas and Hanukkah decorations on our library Christmas tree. The angels you made look just like me! Now I will be a real angel in Cat Heaven.

I would like Ms. Kramm to read you a story called <u>CAT HEAVEN</u> by Cynthia Rylant. I am going to Cat Heaven and see Baker. I have missed him a lot.

It is time for me to go......thanks for being my friends. The Baker and Taylor Fan Club will always have a place in my heart.

Love,

Taylor

Writing Taylor's last letter to the fan club was one of the hardest things I've ever done. Courtesy Jan Louch

Today, Baker & Taylor still produces a cat calendar every year to distribute to libraries across the country. *Courtesy Baker & Taylor, LLC* breath, and nodded to Yvonne. We each grabbed a cat, draped them over the dictionary, and then crouched on the floor so we could prop up the cats by their butts and stay out of range of the camera.

The cats fussed and squirmed and looked off in every direction but straight toward the camera. All the time, the photographer was snapping away, waiting for that millisecond when both cats would look at him simultaneously.

Suddenly, it was over.

<hr />

A month later, a package arrived with a note from Bill.

"What do you think? We love it!" he wrote. "P.S. Enjoy the cat ears!"

Cat ears? We unrolled the poster, which showed a close-up of the cats resting their paws on the dictionary, a clump of pages pushed up between them, with the command USE THE LIBRARY floating between them and BAKER & TAYLOR: *The Literary Cats* in the lower right-hand corner. They looked slightly annoyed, which was no surprise given our various gyrations during the photo shoot.

But for the poster it worked astonishingly well. They looked like they were issuing a stern admonishment to viewers to use the library or else.

We all loved it. The poster captured the dignity and personality of the cats, not to mention that it combined my two favorite things in the world: books and animals.

Yvonne pulled a small box from the package Bill had sent. Inside were several sets of cat ears designed for humans to wear on their heads. We each grabbed one and walked around the library with them for the rest of the day. Of course, some of the patrons wanted a pair too, so we gave the rest away until we ran out. The cats didn't seem to notice anything different, though Baker tried to bat mine off when I knelt down under the circulation desk to get something. Maybe he didn't want any competition for pets from patrons and fans.

Baker & Taylor printed thirty thousand copies of the USE THE LIBRARY poster, produced countless sets of cat ears, thousands of shopping bags with the same photo on both sides, and a slew of T-shirts to give away at the upcoming library conventions. The Baker & Taylor freebies had proven to be so popular at the 1985 ALA convention in Chicago that at subsequent conventions, company sales reps at the booth were ordered to ration the giveaways—one per person each day—or else they would run out of everything before the end of the first day. The promotional items also won two prizes for best freebies at the convention: the shopping bag won for first runner-up while the T-shirt won the title of "Overall Most Terrific Loved by Thousands from Coast to Coast Conference Giveaway Grand Prize."

I was proud, but I wasn't surprised. Shopping bags at any library convention are a vital part of the experience because there are so many bookmarks, and promotional items, not to mention cat posters, and librarians collect piles of galleys—or advance reading copies—for upcoming books. They need something to carry everything in, so a shopping bag is an important part of any library or bookseller trade show.

Most publishers and distributors were already giving away shopping bags with their logos on them at the time, but in 1985 when Baker & Taylor put the cats on the bags, their popularity soon eclipsed every other bag at the show. Their popularity spread like wildfire: the first librarians to carry the bags were stopped by others who wanted to know where they got them. In no time, the Baker & Taylor booth was mobbed and supplies ran low.

Bill sent us a stash of bags, and we kept one open on the floor in the workroom. Baker particularly liked to camp out in the bag; like many cats, he couldn't resist climbing into a bag. But at the same time it was kind of a meta thing, seeing Baker peering out from a bag with a picture of him and Taylor on it.

One afternoon, Baker was snoozing in the bag, and when he woke up he must have forgotten he was in the bag because he was halfway out when he got his head caught in the handle. He took a few steps but the bag still followed him. All of a sudden he got spooked and took off at full speed out into the library. He raced around the stacks, making at least three tours of the library while the bag chased after him. We all felt terrible and tried to catch him, but at the same time it was so funny that we were all in hysterics. Finally he ducked under a chair in the reading room and we were able to cut the bag off him. It took him a few hours to recover, and for the rest of the week whenever we looked at the bag we couldn't help but burst out laughing.

———

Baker & Taylor's cat campaign kicked into high gear in the spring of 1985. In addition to the posters, T-shirts, and shopping bags, the company designed an ad campaign that would run in trade publications like *Library Journal* and *Publishers Weekly*. They didn't use the photos of the cats, but instead artists captured their likenesses in the ads. I had my doubts, but the first series was brilliant: they took famous works of art by Picasso, David, and others and inserted the cats into the drawing or painting. Sometimes it was easy to spot them, other times they were less obvious. And the headline would follow the tone and theme of the art.

For example, one ad had the headline "Are Your Audio Offerings in Tune with the Times?" The artist had used Picasso's *The Three Musicians* but inserted a drawing of a Picasso-like Baker into the lower left-hand corner. Taylor was more difficult to spot. The mustache on the musician to the far right was replaced by a V-shaped upside-down mouth that was clearly feline, with two triangles floating above the head to approximate a couple of cat ears. I laughed because the ad reminded me of how I'd be sitting at my desk typing up reports and look up and suddenly one of the cats would suddenly appear out of nowhere, or I would be looking for them and didn't see them at first, only to realize that there they were, hiding in plain sight.

Other ads in the series riffed off *The Death of Marat* by Jacques-Louis David and an illustration by Sir John Tenniel from early art for Lewis Carroll's *Through the Looking Glass*. I loved the ads. They were clever and funny and I thought they featured the cats in a way that really captured their personalities. Librarians obviously loved the ads, too. But I was surprised when people with no connection to the Carson Valley started to appear at the library, sometimes driving hundreds, even thousands of miles out of their way just so they could meet the cats.

When the first fans showed up in person, we were caught off guard. Of course we were honored, but we also thought it was a bit odd that they wanted to meet the cats in person and have one of us snap their picture with the cats.

Some also brought a poster or shopping bag for the cats to autograph. As I did with the fan mail, I used my rubber stamp for the cats' signature. A few insisted on trying to get the real thing, which of course I refused.

I had assumed that most of the people who visited and those who wrote to the cats were librarians who had gotten their posters and bags from the trade shows, but some regular people started to show up to meet the cats too, as more newspaper reporters and magazine journalists wrote stories about the cats in national consumer publications like *Cat Fancy*. As a result, cat lovers from across the country began to write and visit.

The amount of fan mail for the cats and requests for posters began to skyrocket. We even got long-distance phone calls from people who wanted to speak to Baker and Taylor, which was a big expense back then. If one of the cats was within arm's length, I'd hold the receiver up to their ear so the person on the other end could say hello.

Though we all took turns at the circulation desk, whenever a fan stopped by to meet the cats or called to speak with them, whoever was on duty would come get me or transfer the call to my desk.

"Somebody wants to know about the cats."

I took a breath and launched into my spiel.

"We have two cats, they're named Baker and Taylor, and they live here at the library. They're Scottish Folds, a special breed whose ears crease downward; Baker is a single fold while Taylor is a double fold. They're the official mascots of Baker &

Taylor, a worldwide book wholesaling company to libraries, and Baker likes cantaloupe while Taylor prefers yogurt, and—"

I'd continue and sometimes embellish depending upon whether or not the audience seemed eager to have me continue as well as whether or not something else was going on at the library.

I was always happy to talk about the cats, but the increasing number of visitors and phone calls meant that I was starting to fall behind on my work. One day, after the third interruption of the morning, when another librarian told me to come out to the desk and talk about the cats, I told her I thought she could handle it by now. After all, the librarians were pretty familiar with both Baker and Taylor by then, and they had also heard my spiel enough times that they could recite it by heart.

She agreed, and from that day forward, serving as spokesperson for the cats became part of the job of anyone working the circ desk.

TEN

As more out-of-town fans showed up at the library, so did more locals.

In a small community like Douglas County, the library is particularly important because it's often the sole gathering place where people can meet and hang out for as long as they want without having to buy something. Plus, entrance is free. What's not to love? When I lived in the United Kingdom in the early 1950s, there were small, specialized libraries but they were subscription based. You had to pay a fee to walk through the door as well as check out books. Not so in Douglas County. Anyone could stop by and stay as long as they liked.

And the staff—both human and feline—welcomed them all. After all, public libraries are the most democratic institution out there. We don't turn anyone away; every stripe of people walked through our doors, and of course, still do. Just like public schools, libraries are the great leveler, but even more so because they actively cater to every segment of the population, from kids reading board books to elderly patrons who are researching their family history.

Not only did people look for information in books, but they also turned to us for all kinds of questions that were close to impossible to research on your own back then, just as they'd done in our first, smaller library. For instance, once a patron asked us how long it would take to drive from Stateline, Nevada, to Klamath Falls, Oregon. AAA could help with the details, but you had to pay for a membership. Again, we were free.

So I hauled out a gazetteer—an oversized book of detailed maps covering a specific state or county, for those of you who have never had the pleasure—and traced a piece of string along the twisty, turny roads to come up with close to an exact distance, also giving a rough estimate of the time required to reach the destination, depending, of course, upon how many dogs happened to be snoozing in the middle of the road along the way.

I could have given a ballpark figure, but the patron wanted the exact distance and time; patrons could be funny that way, but then again, so could librarians.

Libraries also provide unfiltered access to information in the form of books and other resources that reflect a wide variety of opinions and ideas. And in the past librarians served as the primary gatekeepers to what was essentially a repository of knowledge.

In my career as a librarian, I've always tried to vet the books, magazines, and other materials that appeared on our shelves through a combination of popularity, cost, usefulness, and whether we already had a similar title on the shelves. Of course, not everyone agreed with our choices, and that was okay, but what disturbed me more were the people who didn't like the fact that the purpose of a library was to provide a wide variety of viewpoints, whether or not you agreed with them.

One day, I was reshelving books in the history section and noticed a piece of paper sticking out of the top of a book about World War II. I pulled it out—it was a brochure—and the words on the cover made me stop breathing.

"The Holocaust *NEVER* Happened," it said in big red letters. I'd recently read a story in the paper about a group of so-called Holocaust deniers that had popped up in the area. I opened the brochure, which was replete with typos, misspellings, and grammatical errors. I checked the other books nearby on the shelf. Same thing. I leafed through each book, pulled out twelve brochures in all, and brought them up to the circulation desk.

"Oh, they've done it again," said Dan.

"They've been here before?"

"Yeah. I actually saw a guy putting them into the books, and when I told him he couldn't do that he accused me of censorship."

"That's not censorship," I almost spat, I was so mad. "It's defacing library property. After all, you wouldn't give a kid a bunch of crayons and let them mark up a book that they didn't like. Why should we let a stupid adult go and stick material into a book that doesn't belong there?"

I loved books so much that I couldn't help but take it personally whenever somebody didn't give them the respect that they deserved. After all, books should be treated like the treasures that they are, not like a garbage dump.

As I tossed the brochures in the trash, I'm sure there was steam coming out of my ears. If you don't agree with something and want to write and publish your own book stating your views, that's fine. Traditionally, public libraries have been very good about finding and putting books with opposing views on their shelves. I mean, we already had a copy of *Mein Kampf* on the shelves, but of course the guy didn't tuck a brochure into *that* book.

Personally, I wouldn't put *Mein Kampf* on my nightstand, but we had it because sometimes people need to find a way to justify their position, whether it's negative or positive. The information should be available. People requested books they wanted to read all the time so they didn't have to buy them; I empathized with them, because I did the same thing. Normally, we'd buy books for the library based on reviews in the trade magazines as well as based on Bill Hartman's recommendations. But if a patron requested a title that was off our radar, then we'd bring it up at the next book-selection committee meeting so that it would be several people who made the decision not to buy a particular book instead of just one person. But really, we were willing to entertain anything.

Of course, as in libraries everywhere, at least once a week someone would come in and ask us to remove a particular book from the shelf. A lot of times, the books people wanted us to remove were political in nature. Either a conservative wanted us to remove every book written by what they perceived as a liberal politician, or vice versa. One patron only wanted us to carry books written by mainstream Republicans.

In fact, it happened so frequently that I had long ago prepared a canned speech whenever a patron complained about a book. I'd take a deep breath and then launch right in:

"Thank you for your opinion, but just like a moderator in a debate, a public library is there to make all matters of opinion available, *blah blah blah,* and there are always more than two sides to every issue, *blah blah blah*, and we appreciate that you've taken the time to come and tell us about your opinion, *blah blah blah blah.*"

Sometimes they'd argue with me, but most of the time they'd walk away and make sure I saw that they were frowning at me the next time I noticed them in the library. Just in case, I made sure to check the book in question for damage and incoherent rants and scribbles whenever it was returned. Occasionally, a disgruntled patron would check out the book and then "lose" it. Of course they'd have to pay to replace the book, and we'd immediately buy another copy.

Other times, it would turn into a game of cat and mouse: a patron would hide a book he didn't like or tuck it into another section, like the cookbooks. We'd eventually find it and put it back.

Once it was actually one of the librarians who insisted on moving a book, and though I disagreed with her, it was funny and, in a warped way, made sense.

I was reshelving books in the children's section when I found a copy of *Mommie Dearest,* the scathing memoir by Christina Crawford about growing up with her mother, actress Joan Crawford. I removed the book and showed it to the staff member on duty.

"What are you doing?" she asked.

"Look what someone did," I said, laughing.

"*I* put it there," she said.

"You did? Why?"

"It was in the wrong place."

"But it's not a book for kids," I said. "On the contrary—"

"But it's *written* like it is." I stopped. To her, it was a matter of literary criticism; she thought it was poorly written—clearly not for adults—and so she decided to move it to the children's section.

She grabbed the book from my hands and made sure I was watching as she put it back on the shelf in the children's section. She dusted her hands off and returned to her post.

Later that day, after she had gone home, I pulled the book again and put it in the Biography section.

The next day, it was back in the children's room. It wasn't the first time she had moved some very unkiddylike books there. But this turned into a months-long ping-pong game in slow motion as *Mommie Dearest* went back and forth between the adults' and children's rooms.

<hr />

Just like our collection, the people who visited the library ran the gamut as well. From the young mothers and toddlers who arrived for story time to the retired business executives who came in each morning as soon as the doors opened and headed straight for the reading room where they could read the newspaper for an hour or two, a cross-section of the community walked through the door every day, and I loved that about the library.

One patron actually bore a slight resemblance to Taylor. He

was going bald in a few places, but a few tufts of hair stuck out at funny angles just like the cat's. His hair was several different colors—just like Taylor's—and his hairline even followed the same shape as the *M* that Taylor had on his forehead.

He even moved like Taylor: he was very catlike and liked to sneak up on people. I'd be in the middle of shelving books and all of a sudden he'd be standing next to me and I'd startle because I didn't hear him. Luckily, there was one way that he *wasn't* like Taylor: at least he didn't sit there and stare at me.

Most of the elderly patrons would come in during the day since many didn't drive at night. A few would drop to the floor the moment they came through the door if Baker happened to be sprawled out on his back near the entrance. The two of them would then spend a few rapturous minutes attending the latest meeting of the Baker Admiration Society, but before long he'd take off in search of new opportunities; that cat wasn't known for his lengthy attention span. Sometimes, the patron couldn't get up by herself, and I'd rush over to help her stand upright again. But that was a small inconvenience; it didn't matter if her hip hurt or his knee had locked up. When they stood back up, they were always wearing a big smile.

And so was I.

Many older patrons weren't allowed to keep a pet, whether because they lived in a retirement community or nursing home, or because they could no longer physically care for an animal and didn't want a cat or dog to face an uncertain future if the animal outlived them. They'd peruse the New Books section and maybe check out a few mysteries, but the main reason that they made the trip was to see Baker. They brought him cat treats paid for out of very limited budgets and would press a few dollars into my hands to help pay for his and Taylor's care. I thanked them and accepted the treats, but I refused the cash. I always felt a little bit embarrassed whenever anyone offered money. I was just happy that the cats made people smile, and in that they served a vitally important purpose for the community.

Not only were the cats instant stress reducers for patrons and staff, but they also helped people make new friends. As the historian of Genoa and a native to boot, Billie Rightmire has written several books on the history of the Carson Valley. She conducted a lot of her research at the library. I occasionally helped her, and we became friends. She always said hello to the cats before settling in for the afternoon, and that's when she noticed a curious thing.

"If I was checking out a book and Baker wasn't at the counter, and someone else came up and asked where he was, it wasn't unusual to strike up a conversation that started with the cats and, more often than not, would veer elsewhere," she said. "Then the next time we bumped into each other at the library or even the grocery store or park, it was easy to say 'Hey, hi, how are you doing?' and you'd have a new friend."

※

And then there was Mr. Figini.

Since we rotated shifts on the circulation desk, I didn't always get to chat with new patrons until they had visited the library a few times or if they came to me with a reference question to research.

One day, I was working the desk when a man who appeared to be in his late fifties stepped up with an armful of books. He looked a bit rumpled and wore the kind of ragged barn coat my father only reluctantly donated to Goodwill after my mother threatened to toss it in the burn pile. He slid his library card over to me and watched intently as I stamped his books: biographies of Jack Benny, Carol Burnett, and George Burns.

He caressed each one that I handed back to him and I flashed back to high school when I watched the mother superior do the same thing, pet her books as if they were, well, cats. "They're due in two weeks," I told him.

"I'll bring them back soon." His voice was stilted and the old floppy hat he wore made it impossible to make eye contact. "I promise."

"Thank you," I said, glancing at the name on his card. *Joseph E. Figini.* "Joseph."

He tilted his head back and I saw his eyes grow wide. "My name is Mr. Figini."

"Mr. Figini," I repeated, but he was already out the door.

He came back a couple of days later, and over the course of the morning I first saw him studying the books in the Biography section and then sitting in the reading room intently focused on the new issue of *People.* Toward noon, he came up to the circulation desk to check out his books. This time he handed me biographies of Sammy Davis, Patty Duke, and Ava Gardner, all in alphabetical order next to each other on the shelf, just like he did the last time.

The same way I used to check out books when I was a kid.

Baker was camped out in his usual spot on top of the computer monitor. Mr. Figini started to pet him but suddenly pulled his hand back, as if he'd touched a hot stove.

"May I pet him?"

"Sure, that's what he's there for," I said. "In fact, his official title is Furry Stress Ball."

But he didn't laugh. He stared at Baker's face as his fingers gently massaged around the cat's ears before moving under his chin. Mr. Figini obviously had some experience handling cats.

He cleared his throat. "My name is Mr. Figini." He said it in the exact same tone of voice he'd used before.

"How do you do, Mr. Figini? I'm Jan." I extended my hand, but he stared at it as his petting intensified. Baker, of course, was soaking it up. He turned his head to the side and his mouth opened slightly. A thin string of drool began to form on a couple of whiskers.

I withdrew my hand and started in on my standard spiel about how Baker and Taylor arrived at the library, but Mr. Figini didn't appear to be listening.

It was clear that he had some type of disability, but he was polite and loved books, and that was good enough for me. After all, it was more than some other patrons could manage on their visits to the library.

When I finished, he nodded politely. Mr. Figini patted Baker on the head and gathered up his books and headed to the reading room where he settled into a chair with a copy of *National Geographic*. After about five minutes, Baker had decided he had held court at the circulation desk long enough, jumped onto the floor, and sauntered into the reading room. He hopped onto the chair next to Mr. Figini, who lightly rested his hand on the cat's back while he read.

They were still sitting like that forty-five minutes later when I headed out for lunch.

The next day, Mr. Figini came into the library, and instead of heading directly for the Biography section or the reading room, he marched right up to the circ desk, where Baker and I were at our posts.

"How are you today, Jan?" he asked.

I almost offered my hand, but thought better of it. "Fine, Mr. Figini, and how are—"

"How's Mrs. Saddler?" he cut me off.

"Fine. Do you want to see her? She's back in the—"

"And how's Mr. Doyle?"

I paused. "He's doing well."

"And how's Ms. Alexander?"

As he continued on through the entire staff directory I nodded and responded with, "Fine." He paused. Then: "How's Baker?"

I refrained from pointing out that Baker was right in front of him and that he was presently scratching him on the head. But hey, I'd go with it. "Fine," I replied, ready for his next question. But he was already finished and heading off to the stacks.

Shortly before noon, he came up to the desk and began his litany, only in reverse.

"Say good-bye to Baker, and Mr. Doyle, and good-bye to—" A look of concern crossed his face. "Is Taylor okay?"

"He's in the back sleeping. Would you like to see him?"

"Oh yes! Where do they sleep?" His voice lost its usual monotone.

"Come on, I'll show you."

As Mr. Figini followed me into the workroom, some of the staffers' eyes widened when they saw him. One person suddenly picked up the phone and started talking animatedly into it. I knew it wasn't because they didn't want to deal with him, but because the various greetings and farewells that were apparently a required part of each visit could eat up a lot of time, time that none of us had to spare. Later on, I saw a couple of staff members cut him off, which made him so flustered that he had to start over at the beginning so he could run through the entire list and make sure everyone was secure and accounted for, including the cats. It was almost like a litany, a call-and-response.

I pointed to their food bowls. "That's where they eat," I said.

"Where do they go to the bathroom?"

"Back here." I opened the door to the closet.

He peered in and nodded. "Today is Joan Collins's birthday," he suddenly announced.

"Is it?"

"Oh yes, she was born in 1933, she's been married four times, her middle name is Henrietta, she has three children named Tara, Alexander, and Katyana, and—"

He was still going when we returned to the circulation desk.

Though I had heard an occasional rumor around town that he was a victim of shellshock, years later I learned that he was a high-functioning but undiagnosed autistic man. When I worked at Camarillo, I'd dealt with a number of patients who were just like him, and indeed, when I saw the movie *Rain Man,*

I recognized many similarities between Mr. Figini and Dustin Hoffman's character.

I rather liked Mr. Figini. We both loved books and cats, and more than a few people viewed us as a bit odd. Plus, he didn't abuse his books, always huge in my world.

Besides, he read the same way I did when I was a kid.

LIBRARY CAT PROFILE: STACKS

Stacks is a brown tabby who has been a dedicated member of the staff at the New Castle Public Library in New Castle, Pennsylvania, since 2010. He has his own Facebook page—Stacks the Library Cat—which he tries to update as frequently as possible.

1) *How did you end up living at the library?*

I wandered in one summer day, and even though the human librarians put me back outside a couple of times, I was determined to stake my claim and wouldn't budge. Fortunately, all it took were a couple of meows and a pitiful look to melt their hearts and take me off the streets for good.

2) *What are some of your jobs at the library?*

I work as the official greeter and kid-magnet for the library. I'm also responsible for taking regular walks throughout the building to ensure that all is running smoothly, and that none of my things have been moved.

3) *What are some of your pet peeves about your job?*

I get upset when humans move my belongings. There is a reason I leave my little mice and ball toys lying around. Also, my coworkers sometimes need to be reminded about filling my food and water bowls in their various spots around the library. Somewhere along the way, I've learned to sleep through the hugs and kisses so human contact doesn't bother me.

4) *Who are some of your favorite patrons, and why?*

My favorite patrons are the children. The adults pay my bills but the children bring me toys, come to my birthday parties, and give me lots of hugs and kisses, so I like them the best.

5) *What's your favorite book?*

My favorite book is *If People Were Cats* by Leigh Rutledge. This book lets people know that if people were cats, "you'd be utterly content just being you." Not to mention that the author lives with thirty cats—my kind of man!

6) *What's your advice for other library cats?*

My advice for other cats is to give the humans a break and show them a little (not a lot of) attention; that way, they'll become your best friends.

7) *Do you have any advice for librarians who'd like to add a cat to their staff?*

It's important to make sure that the library staff, board,

and patrons all welcome a cat into their library. Before I was hired on a permanent basis, the librarians set out a comment book and encouraged patrons to write down their opinions about having a feline employee at the library. After they read through the comments and listened to people give their support, the board of trustees officially brought me on board.

8) *Anything else you'd like to add?*

I've proven to be a great fund-raiser for the library. Bookmarks, decorations, and calendars have all been sold using my likeness. My presence has also brought people to the library for the first time, and they continue to come back. The library staff often tells me how spoiled I am, but I notice that they are frequently looking at me and smiling throughout the day.

ELEVEN

T here's a package for you in the supply closet," Constance told me one morning when I got to work.

That's odd, I thought. Usually my mail—whether it was fan mail for the cats or correspondence about the library—went into the in-box on my desk. Sometimes Bill Hartman sent us extra T-shirts and shopping bags as well as promotional items that didn't go into production for one reason or another.

Or maybe it was a new mug. I glanced at Taylor's Happy Birthday mug alongside his afghan. In his ongoing campaign to distract me from my work, he managed to knock it off my desk at least once a week, though he was considerate enough to do it when it was mostly empty. But the cracks and chips were beginning to threaten the original purpose of the mug, that is, to keep water *in*. A new one would certainly come in handy.

"Why is it in the closet?"

"Because otherwise Baker and Taylor would have ripped the thing to shreds," she replied.

Hmm . . . The cats—primarily Baker—would only attack a package if it contained catnip.

Or cantaloupe.

I opened the closet and pulled out an oversized, overstuffed manila envelope punctuated by a few tooth and claw marks. I squeezed the envelope—it was squishy, not hard, so it obviously wasn't a mug—and read the return address: Jefferson Elementary School in Gahanna, Ohio. As soon as I opened it, Baker and Taylor suddenly materialized. I pulled out a pile of crayoned greeting cards made from construction paper. It looked like an entire class of schoolchildren had each made one. Each card had a drawing of two cats that somewhat resembled Baker and Taylor in terms of color, though some of the kids had preferred to use orange and green. The ears ranged from the proper double fold to nonexistent. One young correspondent had attempted to draw them several times before finally giving up and drawing big black *X*s over them.

I opened one of the cards.

"Dear Baker and Taylor," it began. "My name is Thomas. I am seven years old. I think you are cute. You are probably smart. I want to visit you but the teacher said you lived in Nevada. I changed my mind. Hope you have a good time in the library."

I laughed. Most of the fan mail up until then had come from adults. Even when fans visited the library, the adults were usually more enthusiastic than the kids, who tended to stand shyly off to the side while their parents gushed. Maybe they were embarrassed by this uncharacteristic display of emotion, or maybe they just preferred dogs. This clearly wasn't the case for these kids from Ohio, from the looks of it.

I sifted through the cards for a grown-up's missive and found a small notecard with a pencil drawing of two Scottish Folds on the cover, not of Baker and Taylor, though I recognized the card from a recent cat show. Inside, thankfully, was actual adult handwriting.

The correspondent introduced herself as Leslie Kramm, a second-grade teacher in Ohio and self-professed crazy cat lady and Scottish Fold aficionado.

"I read an article about Baker and Taylor in *Cat Fancy* magazine, and decided to have my class write letters to the cats as a writing project," she explained, adding that she had already written to the Baker & Taylor company to request a couple of posters. Once they arrived at the school, she hung them on the classroom wall and told her students that the cats lived in a library. When they peppered her with questions about the cats, she decided to incorporate them into her curriculum.

For the first lesson, everyone wrote a letter to the cats. Including Miss Kramm.

She enclosed a photo of the class: they held a banner that read BAKER & TAYLOR FAN CLUB while their drawings hung on the wall behind them.

A fan club? I peered at the kids in the photo, with their missing teeth, bandaged knees, and hair sticking out in all directions that their parents had probably carefully combed only an hour or two before. They reminded me of my own kids when they were that age.

Why not? While I read through more of the notes and

drawings, Baker and Taylor had zeroed in on the envelope like a couple of heat-seeking missiles and were busily attacking it. Taylor gnawed on the bottom while Baker had already managed to stick his head inside.

With some difficulty, I extricated the envelope from their grasp and emptied the rest of the contents on my desk. A couple of heart-shaped catnip toys fell out. Of course. Baker pounced on the red heart while Taylor grabbed the blue one.

I hadn't expected gifts. On the contrary, people always expected gifts from us. I was fine with that because I always enjoyed the fan mail the cats received, especially if it showed there was a dry wit behind the other side of the pen. We all laughed a few months ago when we received a card addressed to "The Inmates."

But this clearly stood out: it wasn't just a request for posters or shopping bags from the celebrity library cats. This teacher was serious about using the cats to help teach her students. Who could argue with that?

So I decided to help them.

While the cats proceeded to get thoroughly blissed out on catnip, I wrote a letter to Leslie Kramm to thank her and her students for the effort—and the toys—and that I appreciated what she was doing, using the cats to help her students improve their reading and writing.

I thought back to the struggles I'd had when my son, Martin, was six years old and diagnosed with dyslexia. When he was only in first grade, he scored at the graduate level in logic in an aptitude test, but he hated going to school and was extremely frustrated in the classroom. It was actually his second-grade teacher who helped him and really made a difference in his life.

A few of the students had asked some questions about the cats in their greeting cards, so in the letter I answered a few of them.

"The boys' favorite color is *food*."

"Their favorite books are Garfield anything (their idol)."

"They aren't terribly fast until the can opener comes out of the drawer—but they can be if there is a cricket, spider, or tiny tail-puller in the library."

I folded up the letter and started to address an envelope, but then I paused. What else could I do to help them? I thought of the college students who occasionally called to say hello to the cats. To them, it was a prank. For these seven- and eight-year-olds, however, the cats were real. Maybe they'd take just a little bit more care in their writing assignments if they knew there were a couple of cats on the other end who were actually eager to read their writing *and* write back.

I'd never written a letter as the cats, but why not? I slipped another sheet of paper into the typewriter and gave it a go.

Dear Second Graders,

I glanced over at the cats, who were experiencing the full force of their *Nepeta cataria*—the botanical name for catnip—by lolling back on the floor, their heads and limbs gone completely limp. Baker was actually snoring.

We were so pleased to get your package! In fact, we got so excited that the staff had to lock the package away until our mother came to work.

I wondered if that's what they would say if they could talk. When I was very little, I thought that dogs and cats could talk if they wanted to and that they'd have plenty of interesting news to tell me, but for some reason they decided not to. I never could quite figure it out and it was very frustrating. So I tried to imagine how the cats would address a room full of second graders as well as what the kids wanted to know about a couple of library cats who lived two thousand miles away.

I occasionally heard some of the elementary school teachers who brought their classes to the library talk to their students like, well, they were talking to second graders. I hated when adults did that when I was a kid, it made me feel like they didn't think I was too smart.

It had been a while since my kids were small, but even back then I tended to talk to them as if they were miniature adults. So I decided to write to the Gahanna second graders as if I were talking to my kids when they were the same age.

We do a lot of sleeping and have lots of beds, but we like sleeping in boxes and grocery bags best. We get lots of attention from all the people who use the library, but we don't much like having our pictures taken. I (Baker) like cantaloupe and Tails likes yogurt.

Not many people knew that I had pet names for the cats—Tails for Taylor while I favored Bakey or Bakes for Baker—since I was usually pretty careful about using them in front of the others, but for a group of second graders, well, I figured they wouldn't judge me.

Our mother is going to put all your letters and pictures on our display wall so that the children who come to the library will see that other children know about us. Keep up your good schoolwork and keep on loving animals.

Your friends, Baker and Taylor

Even though I had worn out several rubber pawprint stamps in the last couple of years, I wanted to make these special so that when Leslie passed the letter around the class for the kids to hold and read, they would have every reason to believe that two cats in a library did indeed write and sign it. So instead of just stamping two identical pawprints at the end of each letter like I usually did, this time I did four: two for Baker, two for Taylor. I made Taylor's pawprints look different from Baker's, stamping them with a lighter hand to make them look fainter; after all, he *was* Felix to Baker's Oscar, fussier, and more fastidious. I waved the letter for the ink to dry, and folded and sealed it.

With regard to the pawprint stamp, well, that one action held so much poignancy for me. It was my own decision, my own creativity, and it cemented my connection to a couple of cats who had effectively changed the direction of my life.

I enjoyed writing to the fan club, but I thought that would be the first and last time I heard from them. After all, once they received a poster or shopping bag, most fans never wrote again aside from the rare thank-you note. At the time, it somehow escaped me that the very definition of a fan club meant that there'd be at least occasional correspondence back and forth between the two parties. After all, I was having enough trouble keeping up with the fan mail we already received, not to mention the fans who showed up to meet the cats.

I left the rest of the fan mail for later and was immediately sucked into the vortex of too many things to do and not enough hours in the day to do them. Every year, it seemed like something else was added to the pile. This year, in addition to the budget cuts and a population that kept expanding, the Douglas County school system had recently shifted from a traditional summers-off schedule to a year-round temporary schedule to accommodate the corresponding growth in the number of students attending the public schools. While I wasn't directly involved with the children's section of the library, the change affected all of us. Summer is traditionally a slow time at libraries, but now there was always at least one school in session, usually more. And some of the kids who were on their two-month vacations spent their days at the library because their parents had to work and couldn't afford a babysitter. So we never really got a break.

But I was happy. I loved my job, the patrons, and the people I worked with.

Especially the four-legged ones.

I headed to the post office on my lunch break to mail the letter to the fan club and waved at Mr. Figini as he walked down the street.

I had started to see him walk around town when I was driving around doing my errands on my lunch break. He was as methodical about his walking as he was with his choice of books, and I always saw him at the same place at the same time of day. For instance, if I happened to be driving down Esmeralda Avenue around twelve-thirty, there was Mr. Figini like clockwork. I could set my watch by him. But woe to anyone who disrupted his routine.

Once I asked if he needed a ride.

"Oh, no, no, no, no, no," he replied without missing a step, looking down at the sidewalk the whole time.

"Okay, I'll see you at the library." I waved and drove off. Part of his response could have been due to stranger danger; years later, his niece Claudia Bertolone told me that her mother—Mr. Figini's sister, who had cared for him after their parents died—acted like a protective parent with him, and every day before he left the house, she'd recite a long list of things for him to watch out for and that he shouldn't do. But I think that just like Baker, when he was on a mission he just didn't like to be interrupted. That much was clear when he asked about each of us at the library. And on the rare occasions when I didn't see him at a particular spot at his usual time, I wondered if he was okay.

Which was the same thing he did with Baker.

My lunch hour was almost over so I headed back to the library. I got stuck behind a car from Washington State with an I HEART CATS license-plate frame.

I bet I know where *they're* going, I thought. If only I could hook on to their bumper and coast back to the library, I could save a little gas.

Sure enough, I pulled into the parking lot and followed the woman inside. She literally ran to the circulation desk, and I hustled to keep up.

Baker was camped out on his mat at the circ desk, holding court as usual.

"I love you, Baker!" she announced, loudly enough for everyone in the library to hear.

Not everyone who showed up to meet the cats were librarians; some were what we called Cat Tourists, who traveled around the country—and occasionally the world—on their vacations to meet cats who were famous for whatever reason, however tenuous. Indeed, Baker and Taylor got more than their fair share of these visits. The week before the first package from the fan club arrived, a man actually came all the way from England to visit the cats. Today, Cat Tourists would be gushing about their visit, taking selfies, and posting their photos on Facebook, Twitter, and Instagram. But back then, the only thing they had to work with was a Kodak Instamatic or Brownie, or maybe a Polaroid camera.

While librarians who came to visit often brought their own posters and shopping bags for the cats to "sign," the Cat Tourists usually came empty-handed. But everyone who visited the cats wanted swag—cat swag—to take home as a souvenir of their visit. We loaded them up with posters and shopping bags from our own stash, all of it pawtographed, but they clamored for more. So the Friends of the Library printed up T-shirts and sweatshirts with pictures of Baker and Taylor on them to sell, which helped raise money for the library through the years.

Overall, both cats were pretty much indifferent to fans. While they didn't mind when visitors would pet them and coo over them, they did visibly stiffen if somebody pulled out a camera, which probably reminded them of the professional photo shoots for Baker & Taylor. Their eyes would get big and their ears would flatten: *Are they gonna make me pose?* Taylor would run off, though if Baker was asleep it was obviously okay. You could cause an earthquake and Baker would sleep through it.

TWELVE

———◦•◦———

Life in Nevada has never been easy, even today. After all, the Carson Valley is high desert and extreme weather is pretty much the rule.

Since I moved to the area in 1969, I've seen everything from floods and droughts to blizzards and torrential rainstorms. The vast majority of summers bring relentless heat that make it necessary to draw the blinds, crank the air-conditioning, and relish the time you can sit in the dark cool until you have to venture back out into the blast furnace that waits on the other side of the wall.

For the most part, the weather didn't affect the cats. Aside from visiting the vet, they rarely left the library and definitely preferred it that way.

In February 1986, we were all looking forward to an early spring, including Baker and Taylor since it would bring more birds and bugs jumping around outside for them to stare at. Except during drought years, spring usually brought significant moisture to the valley, between the rivers rising well above normal levels and the snowmelt cascading down off the Sierra Nevadas. But that year a massive flood hit the area, which created havoc for weeks. Power was out at a time when the temperature each night still fell well below freezing. Many ranches and public buildings had generators, but the library didn't, which meant there was no heat for the cats.

Police and emergency workers told everyone to stay home, which didn't much matter since nothing was open anyway, including the library. But I had to get to the cats. Even though I lived only seven miles from the library, nonetheless we were completely isolated in Genoa and cut off from U.S. 395, the only main highway through the area. After making a few phone calls to other staff members, we quickly determined that I was the only employee who could get to the library, albeit by traveling over a lengthy, circuitous back route.

At that point, Baker and Taylor had been without food and water for almost twenty-four hours, since we had closed up early the day before. And despite their thick coats, the lack of heat worried me. And so I set out for the library, and a trip that normally took ten minutes took an hour or more as I dodged roadblocks and navigated flooded and washed-out roads.

When I finally got to the library and opened up the back door, Baker and Taylor were clearly happy to see me, none the worse for wear, though they did seem a bit annoyed. After I spooned wet food into their bowls and they ate, they headed toward the door to the main room so they could get on with their daily routines. They gave me quizzical looks when I blocked their way and quickly closed the door behind me.

"Sorry, guys," I told them. There was no point letting them roam free.

I walked around the cold, dark library to make sure everything was okay. I even checked the book drop and was amazed to find it full of books from the day before, which I thought was a bit ridiculous. Roads were impassable, people were sitting at home in the dark trying to stay warm, but if their book was due that day they'd make it to the library come hell or high water, all to save a few pennies to avoid paying a fine.

I had no choice but to board the cats somewhere else until the power went back on. The phones at the library weren't working, but I had to take a chance that Bob Gorrindo's vet office—which also boarded animals—was open.

With the usual difficulty, somehow I wrestled both cats into their carriers and trudged them out to the car. They yowled the entire way to Bob's.

Indeed, the vet's was open. I dropped them off and headed back home where I waited for the all-clear signal. A few days later, the floodwaters receded and the power came back on. I rescued the cats from their purgatory, and we reopened the library and returned to our normal routine, though it was almost a month before roads in the valley were navigable and debris was cleared. So I still had to take the back roads for a while, which consumed two extra hours out of my day and of course put me further behind at work. I dreamed of getting caught up—just for one day—but I knew that was a pipe dream.

When it came to the weather, we all knew the pendulum would swing back the other way sooner or later. Water has always been a huge issue in the valley just as it has been throughout the state and most of the West. More subdivisions going in meant increased water consumption across the board since many of the new homes had private wells. Though some of the old-timers and ranchers thought that the newcomers—who bought the vast majority of the new subdivision houses—were taking water away from their own groundwater supplies and used the belief to paint all new residents with a black brush, the truth was that the old-timers weren't entirely blameless either, as some of them made a lot of money selling their land to developers. But then again, some didn't have a choice.

I once heard a story that to me perfectly illustrated the disconnect between the new and the old. I knew of a ranch hand who occasionally picked up a couple of shifts at the Carson Valley Inn, and one night one of the managers asked him to write an out-of-order sign and put it on one of the bathroom stalls.

He said sure, and wrote out a sign that said SHITTER DON'T WORK, USE UDDER. I knew he wasn't trying to make a joke. He was a ranch hand, and that was how he thought you spelled "other."

When the manager saw it the next day, he pitched a fit; he was the kind of guy who thought it reflected poorly on him. The ranch hand wasn't fired, but the powers that be kept a close watch on him from that day forward. And they never asked him to make another sign again.

Life was changing rapidly here, and both sides had to adjust. Since the Carson Valley sits right on the border with California, there's always been a lot of reciprocity between the two states. A lot of the people who lived on the California side of Tahoe would come down to Douglas County to go shopping because there simply weren't a lot of retail opportunities on that side of the border back then.

Sometimes the newcomers to the valley who moved here from California lost sight of the fact that they were living in a different state. I was fully aware that it always took a while to get used to an entirely new set of laws and mores when you move. But the people who worked at the county clerk's office finally got fed up with all the people who would come in to register their cars and sign up to vote when they complained, "In California, we didn't have to do this and that." The next time I went to register my car, I saw a handwritten sign on the wall that read, "You are not in California, please don't quote California laws and regulations to us."

Once the newspaper and magazine articles about Baker and Taylor started to appear and letters and postcards showed up, I did what any responsible librarian in my position would do: I started an archive.

I did it for the same reason I saved everything about the Friends of the Library or the building of the new library or anything like that. I saved it because otherwise there was a good chance it would disappear. And then no one would know about it.

I morphed into a pack rat, and tried to save two of every record, including copies of letters to and from fans. A record is very important in history. I've always thought it was wonderful whenever I came across some artifact and I had no idea what it was used for or when it was made and who made it, and then after doing a little detective work in the form of research, suddenly everything became clear. So I thought it was particularly important to preserve everything I could that revolved around the cats. Indeed, soon after I started the archive, I couldn't fit another sheet of paper into the first box, so I started another.

Part of the reason the archives filled up so quickly was due to the Baker and Taylor Fan Club. When another big manila envelope with a return address of Gahanna, Ohio, showed up, at first it didn't connect. But then I dimly recalled a line from the teacher's previous letter.

> *I would like to ask permission to write to you and Baker and Taylor in the future with other classes as I know that an occasional letter from "Baker and Taylor" would mean a great deal to the children.*

I'd forgotten all about it; that and the definition of "fan club." I stuck the package under Baker's nose, but his whiskers twitched and he rolled over and went back to sleep. No catnip this time. So I opened it up, and sure enough, it was a new batch of hand-crayoned feline works of art created by the class of second graders, along with a snapshot of the class.

As I read through each one, I marveled that while the cats had clearly made a lot of people happy at this point, they were also making it easier—and more fun—for a group of seven-year-olds clear across the country to learn.

My own work could wait. I rolled a fresh sheet of letterhead into the typewriter and began.

> *Dear students and Miss Kramm,*
>   *It was nice to hear from all of you and to see your class—you have grown during the last year! Thanks for the drawing of Garfield, Craig, although Baker does not think much of Garfield (competition).*

The kitties have now been here for over five years and are still getting lots of mail and visitors. They play with the string that we use to tie the newspapers for recycling, and make the job much more difficult. They do sleep a lot, like most cats, mostly in our "In" baskets. This makes it hard to get work done sometimes. They also walk on the keys of the computers, but so far have not written anything thrilling, although Taylor did spell PRRRRR.

Have a good school year. Congratulations on all your letter writing, especially to the servicemen. I'm sure they are glad to get your news from home.

Best wishes from Baker and Taylor.

Sincerely,

Jan Louch

The other major contributor to the archives arrived not long after, when I received a letter from a librarian in Minnesota named Phyllis Lahti. In her note, she told me she kept two cats—Reggie and Sadie—at her own library in Sauk Centre, Minnesota, and enclosed a photo.

She floated the idea of starting a club and newsletter about library cats for librarians who already had them, those who wanted them, and for nonlibrarians who were fans. "I would think it could all be immense fun, besides being a way of acknowledging the fine work cats are doing in their respective libraries," she wrote.

I liked the idea, and I certainly could commiserate with the desires of librarians who aspired to have a cat in residence among the stacks. After all, I knew the decision that Yvonne and I had made five years ago happened in a peculiar kind of vacuum: we lived in a very small town where no one would question our executive decisions, and where the community was rapidly growing and changing. In fact, many of the fan letters I'd received from librarians in the last few years also asked for advice about getting a cat for their own libraries. I'd also read several letters to the editors published in trade publications like *American Libraries* and *Library Journal* asking for advice on getting a cat, and every time they'd pointed to the success of our two Scottish Folds.

So I wrote back to Phyllis and said, "Sure, I'm game."

The Library Cat Society launched a couple of months later, and it didn't take long for stories about it to appear in magazines and newspapers. Not surprisingly, the fan mail for Baker and Taylor grew exponentially. But I still made time to respond to every letter; after all, I felt that if someone had taken the time to write a letter to me or the cats, the least I could do is send them a personalized response, even a brief one.

I had it down to a science, much like the spiel that I delivered to visitors at the circulation desk:

1) Thank you for writing to the cats.
2) Yes, we know they're unique.
3) If you want a cat in your own library, we encourage you to get one!
4) Enclosed is the poster/shopping bag/pawtograph you requested.
5) Sorry, the cats cannot be checked out. We consider them to be part of the Reference section, and so they are in-library use only.

I wrote to them as myself, as I felt uncomfortable writing back as the cats except to the young fan club. Besides, I didn't think Baker and Taylor would appreciate me speaking for them, although they clearly didn't want to do it themselves because both cats had always been pretty stubborn. Shortly after they settled into daily life at the library, in addition to angling for scratches under the chin and extra food, Baker and Taylor clearly had decided that their main function in life would be to test the will of every human who crossed their paths. And what better place to do so than a library where there are oodles of people of all kinds wandering in and out all day? One of the ways that Baker liked to test his theory was by becoming one hundred percent immobile as he deliberately transformed himself into a four-hundred-pound cat who absolutely didn't want to be moved under any circumstances. If anyone ever tried to move him from one place to another and he absolutely was not in the mood to move, he'd get a look on his face that I translated as:

"If it's painfully obvious that *this* particular patch of table/carpet/circulation desk is a good place for me to sit and I'm comfortable here, then why is this human picking me up and moving me over *there*?"

I couldn't really blame him; Baker was an entity unto himself. He went where he wanted and did what he wanted, and got very annoyed if you interfered with his progress. I mean, if he wanted to sit on that book, he was unquestionably going to sit on that book.

Taylor was also stubborn, but in a different way. He was a very intense cat. He liked to watch whatever I was doing and would stare and stare, but if I stared back, he'd quickly look away, almost as if I'd caught him doing something bad. He'd even stare when he was in the process of falling asleep. It could be unnerving at times.

But they were both equally obstinate about showing their dismay at anyone who insisted on talking baby talk to them. Some people would come in and say things like "OOOOOO!!! Aren't you just the cutest kitty EVER?" in a voice that was better suited to story time in the children's section. As soon as it started, Baker would just go *scrunch* and try to make himself physically smaller in an attempt to disappear.

Taylor would merely stare down the offender in the hopes that the babbling would stop. I always thought he looked a little embarrassed.

In this, they presented a united front, which wasn't much of a surprise since the cats were fiercely devoted to each other, though it might not have looked like that to a casual observer given their different personalities. Even though Baker spent his time rubbing up against patrons at the circ desk while Taylor preferred to suck up to the staff in the workroom, the truth is that the cats were pretty much inseparable. Not only were they related, but they spent at least twelve hours each day shut in with only each other when the library was closed. One time when Baker had to stay at the vet for a few nights to recover from surgery, Taylor became really upset. He wandered all over the library to look for Baker, and then he actually howled when he couldn't find him.

When Baker came back, Taylor ran toward him; they touched noses, bumped heads, and life resumed.

LIBRARY CAT PROFILE: EMMA

Emma was a Maine coon cat who arrived at the Lyme Public Library in Lyme, Connecticut, in February 2003. Within a few days she was settled in and from that point on she never failed to let everyone know who was really in charge. She passed away on February 27, 2014, but Library Director Theresa Conley—who answered the questions on her behalf—says patrons and staff alike smile when they talk about the antics of Queen Emma, Her Royal Highness, or the Boss, three of her official job titles.

1) *How did you end up living at the library?*

The library put out the word to local animal shelters that they were looking for a cat that would be good in a library setting. The shelter where I was living called the library and said they had the perfect cat. The librarian came and picked me up, and as soon as I set foot in the library, I knew I had found my new home!

2) *What were some of your jobs at the library?*

I greeted people when they came into the library, patrolled the building, and caught more than my fair share of mice. I could also tell when people were sad so I tried to cheer them up by sitting in their laps.

3) *What were some of your pet peeves about your job?*

I liked to sit on the stool at the circulation desk where I could see everything, but the staff made me get down whenever they needed to sit there. Also, my job really never ended; after all, the staff went home at the end of the day, but I was at the library twenty-four/seven!

4) *Who were some of your favorite patrons, and why?*

The ones who brought me treats were always on the top of my list.

5) *What was your favorite book?*

Working Cats of Southern New England by Barbara E. Moss and Melissa E. Moss. There's a chapter about me in it!

6) *What's your advice for other library cats?*

If there are patrons who don't like cats, leave them alone, and if too many little kids are pulling your tail, go hide somewhere until they are gone!

7) *Do you have any advice for librarians who'd like to add a cat to their staff?*

Make sure they know the cat will be in charge. They didn't call me Queen Emma for nothing! But seriously, the staff needs to be committed to taking care of the cat, having someone come in on weekends and holidays to feed and/or dispense medications, clean the litter box, etc. And invest in lots of lint brushes.

8) *Anything else you'd like to add?*

There are so many cats who need homes, and libraries make wonderful homes for them. If the community is receptive to having a library cat, the cat can make the library a happy and fun place to work and visit.

THIRTEEN

———◦•◦———

Life at the library continued as usual: too much work, not enough staff or money. We all dealt with it as best we could.

Regardless of my schedule, I always found the time to write to the fan club.

Many of the letters we received included a question or two aimed at the cats. Some were pretty straightforward, coming as they did from seven-year-olds—Where do you sleep? What do you eat?—while others were pretty off the wall: What's your favorite sport? Do you have to take a bath every night? Did you see *The Lion King*?

The fan club also made it hard to ignore the fact that time was zooming by. It seemed like I'd just finished writing Baker and Taylor's first letter to the new class in September when it was time to send the last letter in June to say good-bye. After all, another school year brought a new batch of members.

I wondered how Leslie Kramm managed; just as she got to

know a whole new batch of kids, it was time to hand them off to the next teacher. I was glad I was a librarian instead; there was more continuity with the stock. Once a new book was cataloged and in circulation, it wasn't going anywhere for years, decades even. And even most patrons tended to stick around for at least a few years.

To accompany the students' cards and letters, Leslie also started to send children's books—mostly about cats—for the library. Patrons often did the same thing, purchasing new books for circulation, often in memory of a loved one, and we always pasted a bookplate in the front of the book to acknowledge the gift before cataloging it and placing it in the stacks. That's what I did with the books from the fan club, typing "A Gift from the Baker and Taylor Fan Club" on a bookplate before pasting it inside.

Leslie told me that class assignments that involved the cats centered around holidays as well as birthdays, but in a kid's world there are holidays and birthdays almost every other week. So we received lots of packages from the club, especially in the fall. First there was an assignment from the new class to say hello, then Columbus Day, followed by Halloween, Thanksgiving, and Christmas and Hanukkah. I realized that it was all in the name of education, and if the kids weren't making pictures of cats out of construction paper and Elmer's glue they'd be drawing pumpkins and turkeys. After I read all of the letters, I gave them to the children's librarian who hung them up on the bulletin board.

Sometimes I felt our exchange was a bit lopsided, and that the fan club sent way more stuff to us than vice versa, though I tried to send new posters and shopping bags to the class as my own stash was replenished. I was always sorry they couldn't just hop on a bus and come out to see the actual cats, but I knew I couldn't take Baker and Taylor there.

One day it dawned on me that just as we saw the cats every day at work and librarians all over the world looked at a poster of the cats each day as they went about their jobs, so did the kids in the fan club. After all, there was a bulletin board in Leslie's classroom that displayed a copy of the current poster along with photos of the cats and several letters from me and the cats.

"The main purpose of the fan club was to have the students practice writing," she told me years later. "And not just the physical process of holding the pencil and correctly forming the letters on the paper, but the idea of conveying thoughts with words. This included brainstorming ideas about what to write, forming complete sentences and using correct punctuation, and learning how to edit and proofread. And creating a little bit of art as well."

It seemed like a lot for second graders to handle, but the cats were obviously helping them learn, so I had even more incentive to write as the cats and get it right.

Dear Class,

We have had some cold weather and some snow. I hide in a grocery bag when a storm is expected and Jan says I'm just as good as the TV weatherperson at forecasting storms.

We keep getting more and more people in the library (and no more staff to help them) and our funds are not keeping up with the economy. Luckily, the cat food keeps appearing in our dishes.

I am getting sort of stiff in my old age, so I have discovered the benefits of sitting under the staff desk lamps, they're warm. All staff get an equal share of my presence, I don't discriminate. Taylor annoys them by LOOKING AT THEIR LUNCH, *and maybe drooling a little. I always thought there was a touch of Garfield somewhere on his family tree.*

　　Love,

　　Baker

I split it pretty evenly between writing to the class as the cats and writing—and signing—as myself. Several times I decided to write just as Baker, don't ask me why; maybe because he was being particularly vociferous about something that morning.

Whenever I wrote to the class as the cats, I tried to think like a second grader. I really tried to talk to them as children but not talk down to them. I assumed that the cats were doing a decent enough job writing back to them because they kept sending cards and letters, and Leslie had told me they were getting better at reading and writing so I continued doing it.

But when I wrote as myself, I had to refrain from going overboard in my attempts to help build their vocabulary by writing something like "To extrapolate the full meaning of cat servitude . . ." It was hard, but I crossed it out and just wrote, "I feed the cats." Not that I wasn't sorely tempted; I've always felt sorry for words that are just sitting around with few people to use them. Like "obfuscate." And I do love to obfuscate . . .

Some of the letters and cards we received from the kids were just hysterical. Once Leslie told the kids to write an essay with the title "My Life as a Library Cat."

"My name is Cocoa," wrote one young student. "It's my job to make sure nobody steals any books or bookmarks or messes up the shelves. The best thing about being a library cat is running around and spinning on the chair. But once I threw up."

Here's another: "My name is Blackie. It's my job to chase the rats and mice away. Then the librarians let me eat them because I did such a great job chasing them down. They taste really good."

I laughed my head off when I read them and then passed them around to the others. But I appreciated what Leslie was doing, because I thought that this was a group of kids who would grow up to love cats and remember the good times they'd had in second grade.

This was hammered home for me when Leslie told me there was a first grader who wanted to be in her class the following year, not because he wanted to have her as a teacher, but because he wanted to be in the Baker and Taylor Fan Club.

⋅⊷⊷⋅

As the cats got older, I worried about their health and wanted them to stay well hydrated. So I actually trained Taylor to drink water on cue. I'd tap his Happy Birthday mug, and even if he was on the other side of the room, he'd come over and take a few sips.

I could also tell him to take a nap, which I did whenever he happened to be camped out on my computer keyboard. I believe that all cats like to sit on keyboards not because they're trying to communicate with you but because they know it annoys you and that you'll pay attention to them.

Even if I got another keyboard for Taylor and didn't hook it up to the computer, he'd still sit on the one that worked. He was one smart cat, but I also think he knew which one was real and which was the con. I don't know if there have been scientific studies to prove why this is the case, but early on I suspected that the truth—and I have to admit it took years of living with cats to come to this conclusion—is that they watch your eye motion, determine the spot that is important enough for you to look at, and make sure to lie down on THE EXACT SPOT so they'd get at least a few head scratches out of your distraction.

So when he got too helpful with the keyboard, I'd pat his afghan and say, "Time for your nap, Taylor." And he'd get off the keyboard and climb onto his bed.

I'd tested my theory countless times, especially with Baker. If he was sitting on a paper or book that I needed, I'd wait until he was looking at my face, then I'd look at another stack of paper for a few seconds. Sure enough, he'd move. In keeping with the charade, I'd huff and moan and throw in the occasional "Oh, Baker," in a convincing tone until he settled down. Then I'd pick up the piece I really needed. But by then, he was fast asleep, secure in the feline knowledge that he had outwitted another human, *again.*

Of course, maybe the cats just wanted to help lighten my load. After all, they knew my workload had increased because I had less time to fawn all over them.

Baker had one favorite trick at which he excelled—aside from eating cantaloupe, which wasn't really a trick—but we never could figure out what he got out of it or why he started in the first place.

We kept a lost-and-found box under the circulation desk, and the cats liked to burrow into the contents. You wouldn't believe the stuff people leave in the library: in addition to notepads and pens, they'd leave shirts, pants, socks, shoes, even underwear. Sometimes the cats would hide or take a nap in the box, but they also used it as a source of toys. Taylor would dive in and rummage around for a while, pull out a shoe or mitten, then happily spend the afternoon destroying it.

One day, Baker pulled a red bootlace out of the box. Instead of wrecking it like Taylor did, he wandered through the library with it, holding one end in his mouth while the other end dragged behind, almost like he was taking it for a walk.

I watched for a while, then picked up the other end of the bootlace. When I started to walk away, he switched to following me like I was taking *him* for a walk. When we got back to the circ desk, I took the bootlace and put it back in the lost-and-found box.

"It doesn't belong to you, Baker, someone might claim it," I told him, though I knew the chance of that happening was about as good as me putting the Holocaust denier brochures back into the World War II books.

The next day, he burrowed into the box, pulled out the bootlace, and looked up at me expectantly.

"Do you want to go for a walk?"

He didn't nod, but I swear that cat was grinning ear to ear when I picked up the other end and we headed off to the stacks for a leisurely walk. He strolled slowly but matter-of-factly, and after we made a complete circuit, after first taking a detour into the meeting room to see if anyone had accidentally left some stray bits of food, he led me back to the circ desk, dropped the lace into the lost-and-found box, and then jumped onto his mat for a nap . . . his third of the day.

After that, we always kept the bootlace in the box and Baker knew it was there, so whenever he got in the mood to go for a walk he'd pull it out. He'd drag it a few feet, and if a human in the vicinity didn't rush to pick up the other end, he'd stop, then sit, before finally throwing a withering look our way as if to say, "Gee whiz, what's the matter? Doesn't anyone want to go for a walk with me?"

If no one volunteered, he'd take the bootlace for a walk by himself. But from the way he was hunched over and dragging his feet it was clear that he wanted to make sure everyone in the library knew that he was not at all happy about going solo.

Baker usually saved the bootlace trick for when the library was pretty empty. He never did it if there were more than a few patrons around, and he only badgered staff members to accompany him. He wasn't ashamed of it, but in the same way that there are certain things you only do or say in front of your family, for some reason he always saved the walk-the-bootlace trick for us.

The cats never ceased to amaze me. We didn't train Baker to walk with the bootlace, he just did it, but only when *he* felt like it. And though Taylor learned to drink water and take a nap on demand, nobody taught him to sit like a Buddha, he just did it.

We didn't want patrons to know the cats could do things like this, because then people would come in and want them to do tricks all the time. And the library was their home, it wasn't a circus.

But some people obviously treated it like one, and worse. What really got my goat were the various items that people used as bookmarks. I didn't mind the letters and birthday and anniversary cards, though I did hope that they left them behind because they simply forgot and not out of malice or because they didn't care. And we'd sometimes find spare change tucked into the book pocket when a patron returned an overdue book after hours and wanted to pay the fine.

But when people used "bookmarks" that clearly damaged the book, that made me mad. After all, I personally believe that dog-earing a page should be a crime, so when I'd find a pencil or a lipstick crammed into the spine, I could feel my blood pressure rise. One time I was checking in a book that had been returned and I found a popsicle stick stuck to the pages.

On two separate occasions, when patrons left a banana peel and the top half of a hot dog bun between the pages, I was sorely tempted to show up at the patron's house with the moldy bun or slimy brown banana peel and say in the most innocent voice I could muster up, "Did you forget something?"

But I always refrained. At least I knew that it wasn't Mr. Figini; he always returned books in better shape than when he checked them out.

In fact, I was so fed up that I would have happily welcomed some kind of electronic bookmark that would magically save your place, which, coming from me, was nothing short of a miracle. Because along with the march of constant development and population in the Carson Valley, all of the technological changes at the library also continued their unfettered march into our apparently Jetsonesque future. Every time a new computer system came through the door, the staff spent weeks, months even, learning each one. Just as soon as we started to feel comfortable with it, *BAM!* something else— invariably touted as the latest and greatest—would come along.

As I've already mentioned, the first major transition at the library came when we switched from a card catalog to the statewide system, which began in the form of CD-ROMs but then morphed to an online network a few years later. It was so hard for some of us to make the switch that we held on to the card catalogs in the main room until well into the 1990s. Part of it was to cover our butts in case the computerized system crashed, and at least this way we'd have a backup. Once it was clear we were not going to be able to return to our caves, we at least recycled the old catalog cards for notepaper and—yes—bookmarks.

Many of us still chose to default to the old tried-and-true low-tech methods whenever we could. Of course part of the reason was because the learning curve in those days was so steep, but I think the issue really came down to the question we asked ourselves almost every day: *Could we spare the time?*

The answer was always no . . . except when it came to the cats. In fact, the cats benefited from the frequent technological snafus that were a natural part of learning any new system but made us want to pull our hair out. For instance, we quickly discovered that our brand-new computerized checkout system was not known for its stability, and tended to crash at least once a week, usually more often. Whenever that happened, we had to stay at the library late into the night to handwrite all of the transactions that had taken place that day. Though we obviously weren't happy about it, it did mean that we got to spend more time with Baker and Taylor, and they of course were happy to have someone stay with them late into the night.

————◦•◦————

It's no wonder that the library was one of Mr. Figini's favorite places. Autistic people need routines and schedules; they're most comfortable when everything is in its place just as they expected and there are no surprises.

Everything was the same every time he came in. After all, a library—*any* library—is essentially just one vast space of orderliness and predictability. The books are always put back in the same place on the shelf, they're arranged in order, and the new issue of *People* is always out on the rack on Tuesday mornings.

And generally speaking, you're going to be treated pretty well. Librarians can be short-tempered and have bad days of course, but if you come in and show that you share our love for books, well, that goes a long way toward softening our harsh edges. And then we'll bend over backward to help you.

No one's yelling out or crying—well, except for the librarians sometimes—and there are no unseemly displays of emotion. It was the perfect place for Mr. Figini to spend time with his beloved books and cats.

And, as it turned out, *trees.*

In 1989, spring had arrived early in the Carson Valley. I glanced out the window one morning, and saw Mr. Figini sitting on one of the benches outside the library. But he wasn't reading, instead it looked like he was just staring at the trees, which were in full bloom.

They were glorious bursts of white blossoms. As usual, I was already running out of time to check off everything on my must-do list for the day, so I headed back to my desk.

A half hour later, I passed by the window again. Mr. Figini was still sitting on the bench gazing at the blossoming trees.

Ah, why not? I thought, and went out and sat down next to him on the bench. He gave a slight nod without breaking his gaze and we sat together for a while, just looking at the trees. If Baker wasn't so afraid of being outside the library, I bet he would have liked to sit with us as well.

I thought Mr. Figini just liked the bright colors, but I also knew better than to ask if there was another reason. Years later, his niece Claudia Bertolone filled me in. Mr. Figini grew up in Los Altos, California, which was then mostly an agricultural area. His dad owned a peach orchard, and built a house on the property.

In those days, children with disabilities were largely hidden from the world and rarely attended school. And among old Italian families, many believed that a child who deviated from the norm in any way reflected badly on the family. He attended elementary school until it became apparent that he was different. Afterwards, he was homeschooled, where he learned to read.

But somewhere along the way, young Joseph proved that he could do a certain kind of job, and he became responsible for irrigating the trees. He'd stand at each clump of trees with a hose, watering each spot for ten minutes before it was time to move on to the next.

"Is it time yet?" he'd yell. His sister—Claudia's mother—would yell back "Not yet!"

A few more minutes would pass, and then she'd yell "Now!" and Mr. Figini would move on to the next clump of trees. There was no irrigation on the property, so it took all day to water the acreage, and he had to start all over again the next morning.

But he loved his job. And when the family moved to the Carson Valley in the mid-1970s, Mr. Figini was left without a job to do. That's when he began to walk all over town and spend hours at the library, and that became his job.

The blossoms were breathtaking. Why didn't I do this more often?

I smiled at Mr. Figini. He nodded slightly, and then smiled back.

FOURTEEN

———◦•◦———

Nineteen eighty-eight was a year filled with change. First, my parents decided to sell their home and ranch in Genoa and head back to California. My kids were both grown and on their own, so at the age of fifty-seven, I moved into the first house I had ever owned by myself.

I could stick my head out the door and see my beloved Sierra Nevadas on one side and the Pine Nuts on the other side of the valley. The house was just a few blocks away from the library, which saved me a bunch of time in the morning.

But new tasks and responsibilities always rush in to fill an existing vacuum, and whatever time I was saving by living in town was immediately taken over by caring for Baker and Taylor as well as my own cat, a friendly and loving Maine coon named Missy Mac. I didn't mind, of course, it's just that sometimes I felt like the Scottish Folds needed a full-time handler or agent to deal with the increasing crowds and visibility.

After I moved into my new house, the first thing I did to

mark my turf, so to speak, was to hang the Baker and Taylor posters on the wall in the hallway. That way, even though the cats were safely tucked in down the road I could still see them and say hi coming and going any time of the day or night.

As my children got older and then left the nest, they obviously became less dependent on me, and as such, I soon discovered that it was very much necessary for me to have some kind of contact with animals both at home and at work. I really felt very strongly that Baker and Taylor were surrogate children in a sense. I had to take care of them, I had to take them to the doctor when they weren't well, I had to make sure they were fed and that their bathroom was clean and so on. It was really very much like having two four-legged children.

I was happy with my new house, but it was a big adjustment for me to make. After all, I was living alone for the first time in my life. Plus, I missed the ranch and my parents. At the same time, it simplified life as well because the library was so close. For instance, on Sundays when the library was closed, somebody still had to spend a little time there to empty the book drop and feed the cats and make sure they were okay. As their primary caregiver, most of the time that task fell to me. But I didn't mind; I liked being there on Sundays. It was quiet, and if there was something that didn't get done the previous day, I'd have a chance to finish it up because there were none of the usual interruptions.

Sometimes I'd come in the back door and Baker and Taylor would be all cuddled up together on the afghan, but other times I felt bad because they'd be sitting by the back door waiting for me when I first pulled up. They were always glad to see me, but after I fed and watered them and scooped the litter box, they wanted to know why they couldn't go out into the library. Taylor would usually glare at me, and Baker would paw at the door, but I couldn't let them go out into the library because then I'd have to go find them and round them up, and they could be quite clever about being not found. It could take an hour or more if they decided to be extra stubborn, and then my day would be shot.

When it came time for me to leave, I'd tell them good-bye and then head to my car. Sometimes I'd look back and there they were, sitting by the back door just watching me, which of course would make me feel horribly guilty. They were people cats; even though they might be ignoring you, they still liked to have you around.

The library was also closed for holidays of course, and because I felt bad about leaving the cats alone for the day, I usually brought in a plate of leftover turkey the day after Thanksgiving and Christmas each year. So did some of the other staffers, so Baker and Taylor seemed none the worse for wear after the time on their own.

But they still let us know that they didn't like it.

Living in town and not having chores to do on the ranch also made it easier to have a social life, that is, if I wanted one. The truth is that by that time I was pretty set in my ways, and I had long ago grown accustomed to having cereal for dinner or turning on the light at two A.M. to read if I felt like it, which was kind of nifty.

The second big change that year was that Yvonne decided to retire. I would miss her—after all, she had given me my big break—but she had been working as the library director since 1965. And once Yvonne left, I would officially become the sole caretaker of Baker and Taylor, which was becoming a bigger job with each year that passed.

We still had a steady stream of visitors who showed up to see the cats each day, but I realized that things had really turned a corner one day when a tour bus pulled up. As the driver approached the desk he was followed by a steady stream of people, and I really thought I knew what he was going to ask.

"The bathroom's down the hall," I said, helpfully pointing the way. It wasn't the first time: these were the days before chain restaurants and McDonald's were everywhere, and U.S. 395 was a long twisty stretch of highway with nothing but scrub brush on both sides for a couple hundred miles if they were heading south into the Eldorado National Forest as many of the tour buses tended to do.

"Where are they?" he said instead, a bit breathlessly.

"Where are who?" I asked, though obviously I knew who "they" were.

The driver saw Baker in his usual spot on the circ desk and he pointed and grew very excited. "There he is!" he announced to the others. "I'll have you know these are some very famous cats!"

Baker sleepily opened one eye and lifted up his head as a crowd of around forty people swarmed the desk. The bus crowd took some pictures, scratched behind his ears a few times, and left. I thought it was pretty amusing, but I braced myself for more to come.

After all, by this time Baker & Taylor had turned the merchandising spigot on full blast. In addition to distributing new posters to tens of thousands of libraries throughout the country, the company was giving away T-shirts, coffee mugs, wristwatches, notepads, paperweights, and the ever-popular shopping bags, which would be handed out by the thousands at library trade shows and conventions on both the national and regional level. Even though I rarely attended a convention, I did hear secondhand reports about arguments breaking out between librarians over the last shopping bag in the booth. The company had also ordered a pair of custom-designed human-sized costumes modeled after the cats. Baker & Taylor had commissioned them from the Walt Disney Company and they made their debut at the American Booksellers Association convention that spring, where convention attendees could have their photos taken with the cats. They were a huge success, and soon a librarian's show would not be complete without a photo taken with the official Baker & Taylor mascots.

"It was tchotchke heaven," Jim Ulsamer, the former president of Baker & Taylor Books, told me years later, still a bit stunned by the success the cats brought to the company. "It seemed like we couldn't overdo it, because no matter what we produced, the librarians just ate it up, they couldn't get enough. Whenever I visited a library, a poster was there. Think about it: you're a librarian and spend hours in the library five days a week, and every time you look up our company is advertised in a nice and warm way.

"Our competitors *hated* those cats," he added with a grin.

Tchotchke heaven, indeed. We got a lot more visitors, especially from the Bay Area of California because it was an easy day or overnight trip from San Francisco. Or else fans would be traveling to Reno or Lake Tahoe anyway and think, "Oh, that's not very far from where Baker and Taylor live, let's go see the cats."

Occasionally, visiting librarians would grill me about our

relationship with the company, mostly to find out if we were getting any special deals on books. Some didn't believe me when I told them that we weren't, and they'd say, "If only I got a dog and named it Baker or Taylor, I could have really cleaned up," loud enough for everyone to hear.

Yvonne and I finally realized how popular the cats really were on two separate occasions, both thousands of miles away from Minden. First, just before she retired, Yvonne traveled to a library convention in London. When she was browsing the booths on the trade-show floor, she casually told someone that she worked at the library where the Baker & Taylor cats lived.

Within minutes, she was mobbed by people, both librarians and exhibitors. They peppered her with questions about the cats and asked for her autograph.

Not long after, I was in Boston on vacation to visit my brother and his family. I dropped by the Peabody Institute Library in nearby Danvers all prepared to spend a few hours happily immersing myself in their research library. But when I got there, the librarian told me that it was closed to the public until the next day. I was disappointed and turned to go, but then I remembered how the librarians had reacted to Yvonne in London. So I decided to play the cat card.

"Oh, I'm sorry to hear that," I told him. "You see, I'm a librarian and I've traveled all the way from Minden, Nevada, to see your collection, and—"

He suddenly sat up straight. "Minden? You mean Minden where the cats live?"

I tried hard to hide my smile. "Yes, do you want to see my business card?"

He stood up and swept his arm out to the side with a great flourish. "Oh no, that won't be necessary, of *course* you can come in, in fact, I'd be honored to provide you with a personal tour of the premises. Is there anything in particular you'd like to research? I can let you into our special collections if you'd like."

Suddenly, the world—or at least the Peabody—was my oyster.

I grinned the rest of the day while he asked me questions about the cats. Yvonne was right. This thing had taken on a life of its own. But I couldn't help but realize that the cats remained largely oblivious to it all. After all, to them it was perfectly normal that their home happened to be a library where a constant parade of people wandered in and out all day. It was the only life they knew.

The cats were the center of attention, which is just as it should be. But every so often, a patron or visitor would treat me like *I* was the main attraction, at which point I'd quickly steer their attention back to the cats. I liked the idea of the cats having the exposure and making people happy, but I was perfectly content with my spot behind the scenes. Although I loved how the cats had changed the library and made it a great place to work, we hadn't done this for ourselves, we'd done it because it was good for the library. And sometimes people lost sight of that.

◆◆◆

In January 1988, the contract that we had signed with Baker & Taylor three years earlier expired. We renewed our deal with the company with a one-time payment of $5,000 that would ostensibly cover the rest of the cats' lives, though the agreement didn't specifically mention that the deal would expire when the cats did. In reality, that meant that Baker & Taylor could continue to use the cats after their deaths—which indeed is just what happened—though Bill had already started to drop hints that the campaign was so successful that the company would pay to replace the cats when the time came. But Yvonne and I didn't dwell on that because we felt we'd deal with the issue when we were forced to. After all, the cats weren't even ten years old yet.

But a new contract meant another photo shoot, which we all dreaded for the cats' sake. We signed the contract, banked the check for future expenses involving the cats, and waited for the photographer to show up.

In the meantime, the library board of trustees began reviewing résumés and interviewing candidates to replace Yvonne as library director. Some of the applicants clearly wanted the job because it was the home of "the famous library cats," while others simply viewed it as a job, nothing more, nothing less. But for the benefit of the cats, we all—staff and board members alike—believed that the new director had to be a cat lover, otherwise it could make for an uncomfortable working environment for everyone involved.

With that in mind, we narrowed our scope. One résumé stood out: Carolyn Rawles, a librarian from Indiana. In her cover letter, she mentioned she was looking for a job on the West Coast so that she could be closer to her family. She'd gone on a few interviews, she wrote, but nothing appealed until she saw the ad for the job in Minden. "That's where the cats live!" she said.

We invited her to come out for an interview, and she told us that both patrons and staffers at her library in Indiana became very excited at the prospect of her going to work every day with Baker and Taylor. "Though they'd miss me, I think they were a little more inclined to let me go, knowing I'd be working in Minden," she confided.

During the interview process, maybe one percent of me wished I'd be hired for the job of library director. Although I had been second in command at the library since Yvonne first hired me, we both came on board at a time when you didn't need a college degree to get a library job, even for a director's position. Later on, that changed when the state and most towns and counties started to require an advanced degree in library science as well as several years of experience working in a library.

But I wasn't terribly broken up, because honestly, I didn't really want the job in the first place. I had witnessed Yvonne's frustrations firsthand as she dealt with everything from budget cuts to county politics, which meant that she spent very little hands-on time with books, or with the cats for that matter.

The primary reason why I wanted to work in a library was because I wanted to be surrounded by books, though of course the job itself didn't leave me with a lot of time to read. But at least I could talk about books with patrons and the other staff members. If I were to be in charge as the director, my life would change, and I knew I wouldn't be able to spend as much time with the cats.

In fact, I actually got a taste of Library Director Hell when I served as interim director for the six months after Yvonne retired—and before Carolyn came on board—and I had to attend county meetings, which were little more than endless exercises in small-town politics. I've always hated having to fight for things and listening to people argue endlessly. It was especially difficult to remain civil when somebody would suggest cutting two or three people from the library staff as if it was as simple as getting a haircut. Plus, it's very hard to be in a job when you know you're not going to stay. Essentially I was a placeholder, just waiting for the next person to come along while I held all the responsibility for keeping everything going.

I liked being second in command better because I could breathe. First, because I didn't have to attend any meetings, but also because I could focus on projects that actually made the library a better place, from building up our special collection of Nevada history to culling outdated reference books.

I also didn't have to be constantly reminded of how perilous our budget really was, though this is one case in which the cats definitely helped. Before the cats arrived—and before the new library was built—I think that county officials considered the library to be little more than one big room with a lot of books on the shelves, where their kids did their homework after school. While I don't think that Baker and Taylor had any influence on the budget from one year to the next, user attendance and circulation did increase, and that helped make the county officials more aware of the library. You know, "The cats are in the paper again for the third week in a row," didn't hurt.

But of course, nothing was ever guaranteed, and the constant uncertainty was unnerving. Although the book budget had been restored since the drastic cuts of 1983, it felt like we were still playing catch-up more than five years later, which is another reason why I was happy to be second in charge and remain behind the scenes. When it came to the budget, the only things I wanted to know about were more concrete: Can I afford to buy this for the reference collection? Do I have time to deliver books to homebound patrons? In a way, running a library is like running any business, I understood that. But on the other hand, there were definitely aesthetic concerns as well: Is this going to enhance our collection? Can we bring in authors for signings? Is this particular section of the nonfiction collection lacking something?

Though we all liked to complain about the nonstop nature of our jobs, no one could deny that having a couple of cats made things much more enjoyable.

After Yvonne retired and moved to Washington State, I was mad at her for a long time. After all, she was my close friend and coworker and we had a lot of history together. She was very supportive at work and always listened to any ideas or problems from the library staff, we had a lot in common, and had a lot of fun at work and outside as well. She always got first dibs when a new mystery by one of our favorite authors came in, but I didn't mind because I knew I'd get it sooner or later.

Now that she was gone, I was first in line for the new mysteries, but it didn't matter. I missed Yvonne.

When Carolyn started working at the library, I gratefully stepped down as interim director to resume my place as second in command, which meant resuming my share of responsibilities at the circulation desk. Sitting at the desk, my coworkers and I became the human face of a public institution, and it wasn't uncommon for people to come into the library and just unload. Like me, most of my coworkers were not big fans of confrontation. But if somebody came in and started to give us a hard time, we had to be patient and listen to their complaints, whether or not they were justified. And sometimes they could get quite heated. When they left and we'd done whatever we could to defuse the situation, from promising to consider ordering a particular book to making sure the ficus plant was watered, I know I wasn't the only staff member who'd escape to the workroom to find the nearest cat. Spending a few minutes to pet Baker or Taylor—maybe both, if you were lucky—while relaxing with a cup of coffee was just about the best stress-reduction method around.

The stress relief didn't end when I left work at the end of the day and headed to my new home: Missy Mac would always meet me at the door and do her best to welcome me home.

Missy Mac loved to make me happy. When she sensed that I'd had a bad day, she'd go out in the yard and catch a few rodents, mostly voles. Once, after I'd had a nothing-had-gone-right day, she went out and caught and killed twenty voles, lined then all up on the front porch, and then meowed at me to come out and look. I was very proud of her, and I completely forgot the stresses of the day. Missy Mac knew what she was doing.

I had cats at home and cats at work, and in each place I was surrounded by books.

My idea of heaven.

For the first time in a long time, I had no conflict in my

life. Everything was just the way I wanted it, a sweet spot. Of course, like most people, I would have been happy with more money, but to me the absence of conflict—at work and home— was far more valuable to me.

Even though the cats had been at the library for over five years, I was still learning things from them, like the importance of having something akin to a stress ball to reach for when things got tough. After all, they *were* furry stress balls. They also taught me that everyone needs something that can serve as a distraction and help to quickly resolve conflicts and calm everyone down to make life smoother at work, and home, for that matter. If that happens to be a couple of cats then fine and dandy. For someone else a couple of dogs would have worked better, or a gecko. Who knows?

Baker and Taylor could have used a couple of stress balls of their own when it came time for yet another photo shoot on May 9, 1988.

The marketing team showed us mock-ups of the kind of campaign they had in mind, which showed the cats sitting on a shelf acting as a pair of bookends to hold up that season's new books. The caption for the main poster read "Snuggle up to a good book." It looked like Baker and Taylor again would be required to execute a series of poses every which way, which I dreaded. As expected, as soon as the photographer started to set up his camera and lights, the cats vanished into thin air. After all, they knew what that equipment was for. When we found their hiding spots and then pretty much dragged them out in front of the camera, they acted up immediately. "Oh ho,

I remember doing this before, and no way are you going to get me to cooperate," said their body language. "I'm just going to sit here and look snarly."

And they did.

The third time was definitely *not* the charm. The photographer tried everything, and we helped as usual by shaking a garden variety of cat toys and tossing over the occasional cat treat, but Baker and Taylor would have none of it. Back then Photoshop was merely a twinkle in the eye of its inventor, and the graphic design and editing software that did exist was pretty primitive, so it was still up to the photographer to do most of the work. Today, you could edit out the raised fur on the back of Baker's neck that almost made him look like he had a Mohawk, or make Taylor's eyes bigger so it didn't look like he was hissing when the photographer cooed "Nice kitty!" at him.

But it was a long tough slog, and we all hoped that despite the cats' tantrums, there'd be more than enough good shots of the cats for a decade's worth of ads, shopping bags, and calendars.

I wasn't holding my breath.

Sure enough, a couple of weeks after the shoot, I received a note from one of the art directors to request yet another photo session because some of the pictures of the cats were "less than optimal," as he put it. However, someone else at the company must have warned against it, perhaps figuring that the results from another shoot would be even worse. As it turned out, it must not have been that big of a problem because I didn't hear anything more about it.

That was the only time that the cats really chafed against their celebrity.

BOB GORRINDO, D.V.M.

————◦◦◦————

Dr. Bob Gorrindo was the primary veterinarian who treated Baker and Taylor from when they first arrived in Minden.

When I first arrived in the Carson Valley in 1973 to begin working as a veterinarian, the practice of cats was starting to change in the region. Back then, if you were a cat and you were five or six years old, that was really old. The primary industry at the time was agriculture and ranching, and the only reason why anyone would keep a cat around here was for rodent control. Life on a farm was hazardous, and most farmers and ranchers would just say, "Doc, why would I want to spend ten bucks on this cat when I've got a barn full of cats just like him?"

In the 1970s and 1980s, when people were just starting to move up here from California, they felt differently about their pets. In fact, the entire culture was starting to shift from where cats and dogs were just landscape material to being thought of as members of the family. And when Baker and Taylor landed in town, even though Jan had been living here for over a decade, she obviously regarded them in the same way.

This changing attitude toward cats really changed the nature of my practice. The newcomers treated their animals well and they gave me carte blanche to treat them regardless of how much it cost. More cats were living most—if not all—of their lives indoors, which was new for everybody.

Back then, purebred cats were extremely unusual around here, and I think Baker and Taylor were the first Scottish Folds in the Carson Valley. Whenever Jan brought them in for an exam, one by one, my staff would poke their heads in the room and check them out because of the ears. Nobody around here had seen any Scottish Folds at that point. Then once the cats started to become famous, other people who were at the vet with their pets would stare at them and ask, "Aren't those the library cats?"

Once the posters came out, we displayed them all over the office. I hung the first one in an exam room, another down the hall, and the third in a second exam room. The posters were very cool because little kids who came in with their pets liked to look at them. When a patient had to wait for me or a vet tech to come in the room, it was something pleasant to look at and helped them to relax a little bit, which hopefully they were able to convey to their pets.

Baker and Taylor were very stately, and they had real presence. They didn't shy away from people. They were very comfortable. Once they got to see me, I don't remember them being afraid. I thought they were very cool guys.

They weren't difficult to deal with compared with some cats. After all, it's up to you to decide how difficult you want to make your encounter with a cat. If you want to get into an argument with a cat, it's very simple: you tell him what to do and it all ends right there. But if you let the cat tell *you* what to do, well then, there's no problem at all. My deal with cats is really pretty simple: if I'm doing something to a cat, he gets two very easy escape routes with no impediments. So if he wants to jump off the table, I'll pick him up again. If he wants to run away, that's fine. What you don't do to a cat is grab him and force him to do something he doesn't want to do. Then you're toast, whether you're a vet or not.

Even though people were keeping their cats safer by the 1990s, a twelve-year-old cat was still pretty old back then. That's like an eighteen-year-old cat now, because we simply weren't as knowledgeable as we are now about keeping these guys going.

Baker and Taylor were celebrities in the community. It was like having a retired NFL quarterback living in your community, and because I was their vet it also made me a little bit famous.

FIFTEEN

At the circ desk, we all got used to hearing Mr. Figini ask after everyone's health before he headed off to read some magazines or to check out the biography collection.

I don't think I was imagining things when I saw Mr. Figini soften a bit whenever he looked at the cats. Sometimes I'd catch him standing in front of Baker and just staring at him for a few minutes. I got the sense that he was asking Baker *How are you feeling? Are you okay?* only without saying a word. In that way, he was like Taylor, almost telepathic.

But Mr. Figini was more like Baker in the way that the cat was an absolute slave to routine: now it's time for breakfast. Now it's time to go potty. Now it's time to go stroll up and down the aisles. Now it's time to jump on top of a shelf. And if someone happened to interrupt his quest, he'd glare at the offender and stalk off to wait until the coast was clear.

Mr. Figini understood the cats, that much was crystal clear. He didn't know how to connect with adults—in fact, I rarely saw him talk to another patron, only with the staff—but animals were a different story.

In a way, I also had a lot in common with Mr. Figini: books and cats were just about our favorite things in the world. The only difference was that books had long served as an escape from the world for me, while for Mr. Figini they were his reality. Like me, he loved information and knowledge, and he had an amazing memory. I thought of him almost like a file cabinet: push a button by asking a question and out he'd come with the answer. Over time, he asked us about our birthdays and anniversaries and the names of our kids and pets, so when the appropriate date arrived, he was always the first to say "Happy Birthday" or "Happy Anniversary." Part of that was because of his memory, but part was also because he thought maybe there'd be refreshments.

The children's librarian would put out treats for the kids and Mr. Figini would suddenly appear, especially if there was candy involved. Red licorice was his favorite.

The cats were the same way. They'd prowl around during story time or a lunchtime gathering in the meeting room, all in the hopes of finding a few stray scraps of food. In fact, the only time Mr. Figini strayed from his schedule and came to the library in the afternoon was when there was a special event and refreshments were being served.

It was also clear that he wasn't comfortable with any emotional displays, good or bad, either his or others'. Once, a patron standing in line behind him heard him ask after the cats, and she tapped him on the shoulder. "I just love the cats!" she gushed. "Don't you?"

Mr. Figini recoiled with a look of horror on his face, and

ran out of the library without finishing his list of questions or checking out any books.

Then again, not too long after that, I saw another patron standing behind him interact with him in a totally different way. "Hello, Mr. Figini," she said.

"Oh, hello, Mrs. Grant," he said. "How is your husband? How is your mother?" He kept going, asking the same kinds of questions he asked me and the other librarians. She answered "Fine" to each one, the same way we did.

"He crashed my wedding," she told me after he left.

"Really?"

"Yeah, but it was okay," she said, as I slipped a date-due card into the pocket of her book. "He just wanted some cake. Somebody told me that he'd read the newspaper and find out where there were retirement parties or grand openings, and he would show up just to get some cake."

One afternoon, Bill Hartman showed up unexpectedly. "Did you see this?"

He slid a copy of *American Libraries* magazine toward me. In the publication's annual poll, one of the questions asked readers who they thought would make the best head of the Library of Congress.

Baker and Taylor—the cats—topped the list.

"Well, I'm sure it wouldn't hurt," I said, handing him back the magazine as the phone rang.

"Douglas County Library, how can I help you?" I gestured to Bill to take a seat while I finished up my shift at the circulation desk. For the next twenty minutes, I checked out books, answered patrons' questions, and made change for people paying their overdue fines. I also updated several patrons on Baker and Taylor's activities since their previous visits, launched into my standard spiel for a visitor who'd driven two hours out of her way to meet the cats, and scratched Baker behind the ears whenever I had a hand free.

In other words, it was business as usual at the library.

When my shift ended, Bill came over to chat. "You're the ultimate hostess, you know?" he said.

I let out a snort. "What are you talking about?"

"I was watching you at the desk," he said.

"Pretty boring, huh?"

"No, on the contrary, it was like you were performing an intricate dance," he said. "You never stopped moving, and you made sure that everybody got what they wanted, whether human or feline. You were nothing but congenial and always happy to talk about the cats. Like I said, the ultimate hostess."

"It's my job," I said, making sure he was watching when I shrugged and rolled my eyes, though I did agree with his analogy. Most of the time, it felt like every day at work was one long improvised mash-up of pirouettes, tangos, and two-steps with more partners than I could count. Sometimes the dance went on for hours, but most often it was just a minute or two, if that.

"But you don't have to do it," he said. "That's not why you decided to work in a library. And I can tell you that there are plenty of librarians who would simply give the canned speech and nothing more."

"Maybe so, but it's made the job easier."

"All I know is that you've changed from when I first met you."

I hated whenever people said things like this about me. I knew he was just paying me a compliment, but I always felt a bit protective of my job and worried that someone would show up someday and tell me, "Sorry, you have to leave. You like your job too much."

But I decided to play along. "In what way?"

"When you first started working at the library, you were a bit hesitant, which could be expected since you were still finding your way in the job. But now, you're sure of yourself, you take no prisoners, and—"

He paused.

"What?"

"You actually smile now. Before you didn't."

I quickly changed the subject, and we chatted about upcoming books and library gossip. But Bill's comments were on my mind the rest of the day. I'd be the first to own up to the fact that I still woke up every morning amazed that I got to work with books and cats, and that more surprisingly, I loved my job and my life. It was a far cry from when I first moved to Genoa and I was living in a complete fog.

Even I had to admit, I'd come a long way in twenty years.

Bill wasn't the first to mention it, either; something was obviously in the air. My brother had called a few days earlier, and we spent some time catching up. Suddenly he paused.

"Are you there?" I asked.

"You're laughing."

"Of *course* I'm laughing, what do you expect?"

"It's just that I haven't heard you like this in a long time."

"Like what?"

Another pause. "Like you're back."

"From where, outer space? I haven't gone anywhere."

"But you're *laughing*," he said. "Do you know how long it's been since I've heard you laugh?"

Then it was his turn to ask, "Are you there?"

"Of course I'm here."

"You're back," he then repeated. "Looks like the library saved you, the *cats* saved you."

I couldn't think of a suitable response. "You're just jealous," I finally managed.

And just like that, we were back to our old ways, trading insults and laughing the entire time. Of course I won't go into the details because it's like Baker's bootlace: for family only.

After I hung up the phone, I started to wonder. What on earth would I be doing today if (*a*) I hadn't gotten the job at the library, and (*b*) we'd never gotten Baker and Taylor . . . or any other cats, for that matter?

I knew my life would look quite different. And who knows? I might still be living in that fog.

Deep down I hated to admit it, but I knew Tony was right.

After Bill left, I turned my attention back to work, where a different, more intricate part of the dance was on my list for the afternoon. As usual, the cats had a hand in helping out.

Once a month or so we changed the exhibit in the glass display case in the main room, which usually revolved around a holiday or seasonal theme. Often some of the items on display were family heirlooms that people let us borrow, so I was careful about locking it up when I was finished. Because Baker and Taylor couldn't get in, the case turned into a place of feline mystery and the cats wanted nothing more than to explore it. So we also locked it up to keep them from getting in. But I swear, all I had to do was rattle the keys to the case and Baker and Taylor would come running.

The moment the door was opened, they'd tunnel right in while I removed any items that might not stand up to an extra bit of feline scrutiny. They'd sniff around a bit or bump a paw against the glass case, before curling up and falling asleep as I tried to work around them. There was a fluorescent light up high on the inside of the case, but since it didn't throw off much heat that wasn't the reason why they loved the case so much. I think Baker just loved to be in enclosed spaces and he considered the case to be simply a larger kind of shopping bag, but not the kind he could get his head stuck in.

Both cats also loved to sneak into the mechanical room down the hall, where the furnace, water heater, and cleaning supplies were located, probably because it was open even less often than the display case. Sometimes the janitor had to get in there while the library was open or a repairman came to work on the heating system, and you'd think there was a giant stash of high-grade catnip in there the way Baker rushed toward it the moment the door was propped open.

At first, whoever was in there wouldn't notice the cat. But after a minute or so—I could almost set my watch by it—I'd see a pair of hands holding Baker pop out from the door and deposit him in the hall. And then the door would abruptly close.

Taylor was a little bit different. He definitely could see the merits in an occasional shopping bag, but he was actually a bit claustrophobic compared with Baker's agoraphobic side. One of his favorite things to do was to sit in the middle of a totally empty space, arrange himself in his Buddha pose, and just stare. If someone started to pet him when he was sitting, he'd get up and walk away. After all, you don't interrupt somebody when they're meditating.

Everyone loved Baker because he was so friendly, but whenever Taylor turned his attention your way it made you feel special; he was pretty picky about who he graced with his presence because he did that so infrequently.

⋅❖⋅

By the end of the day, I was usually so exhausted that I was happy to head home, throw together something quick for dinner, and then plop down on the couch with a book and Missy Mac. I was surprised at how quickly I got used to living by myself. I loved my job, of course, but I also loved my refuge at the end of the day. I missed my parents—though I visited them in California—and sometimes I still missed the sheep, cows, goats, and chickens on the ranch.

My daughter Julia had an uncanny sense for knowing just when I was missing them most. After all, she had inherited my animal-caretaking gene, and she lived close by with her own menagerie of livestock to care for.

One Saturday night, I was all nestled in for the evening when she showed up with a box of orphaned lambs in one arm—known as bummers—and a carrier of baby bottles in the other. I peered into the box, and two little faces and tongues bleated back at me. They were swaddled in baby blankets.

"Don't tell me, let me guess," I said.

"Can you babysit tonight?"

"I thought you'd never ask," I said. "Go, they'll be fine."

I let the lambs out of the box and they instantly turned into Velcro; it felt like I was being followed around by two little clouds constantly yelling, "Mom! Mom!"

After I fed them, they nestled in around me on the couch while I ate my dinner. I couldn't read because they never stopped squirming and *baa*-ing and competing for my attention. So I finally put down my book and turned on the TV.

They immediately settled down and stared at the screen. They were mesmerized and didn't even get up to follow me when I left the couch. We were all still wide awake watching *Saturday Night Live,* which seemed to be their favorite, don't ask me why, when Julia showed up sometime after midnight to pick them up.

It felt good, and familiar, but I had no desire to go back to that life. I had created a brand-new one for myself. I was in a different place. But for one night it was perfect.

SIXTEEN

———◦•◦———

It had been a tough morning. I had to run a few errands before work, and I had run into one delay after another. I worried that Baker and Taylor would be hungry. By the time I reached the library, there was no place to park.

When I finally got through the door, I was about to start railing at someone, but when I saw the telltale overstuffed manila envelope from the fan club on my desk, my mood instantly turned around.

The cats had ignored it, which meant no catnip toys. But it was still bulkier than usual. I upended it onto my desk and a pile of cards fell out. The cards all said HAPPY BIRTHDAY! on the front. Yet another holiday: I must have mentioned to Leslie that we were going to have a party to celebrate Baker's tenth birthday.

There was also a videotape in the package. A video? I headed for the meeting room, popped the tape into the VCR and hit play.

Suddenly, a grainy picture of the fan club appeared on the screen. I heard a few opening chords from a piano offscreen, the kids all inhaled deeply, and then started singing.

> *Baker and Taylor are library cats,*
> *They're literate felines and that is a fact,*
> *They live among volumes of books on the shelves,*
> *And love to read stories all by themselves!*

Leslie had mentioned in her last letter that she had a surprise for me, but I had no idea what to expect.

The kids launched into the next verse when Dan and Constance poked their heads into the room. "What's that?"

I hit pause. "It's from the fan club."

"They wrote a song?" asked Dan.

"Leslie did," I said, and hit play.

Second graders are not among the most articulate people, but I was still able to catch some of the lyrics.

> *Their ears are folded like caps on their heads,*
> *So they always look ready to jump into bed.*

Wow. Leslie had really gone all out. Plus, the tune was catchy. It was written in three-quarter waltz time with a melodic range that a seven-year-old could manage. I noticed that I wasn't the only one swaying back and forth on the first beat of each measure.

We reached the end of the song. Leslie had tucked a comb-bound songbook into the package, so I hit rewind and this time we all followed along.

> *Gray and white Baker likes to lie in the sun,*
> *Or under desk lamps (but that's not as much fun),*
> *He forecasts bad storms just like weather men do,*
> *But by hiding in bags! (But a box would do, too!)*

"How come they know so much about the cats?" asked Constance.

That's when it dawned on me: while everyone—staff and patrons—knew about the fan club because we hung their artwork and letters up on the walls and displayed their handmade ornaments on the Christmas tree every year, they had no idea of the extent that I was corresponding with the club.

The verses Leslie wrote must have come straight from my letters. I dug my letters out of the archives, and sure enough, that's just what she did.

In one letter, I wrote the following to the class:

> *Baker has developed a fondness for sleeping on an adding machine—not a very comfortable spot, but he likes it. Maybe the numbers are seeping into his brain. Taylor devotes most of the day to trying to move dinner hour up earlier and earlier. He is a true oinker.*

A couple of months later, Baker wrote this:

> *We have had some cold weather and some snow. I like to go into a grocery bag when a storm is expected; I think I'm just as good as the TV weatherperson at forecasting storms. We need more, both for skiing and to break the five-year drought.*

I thought the kids were absolutely adorable before, and now, the video made them irresistible. I just wanted to hug them all.

———◄►◄•►———

As the fall of 1991 arrived, it was hard to believe that Baker was about to turn ten years old. Of course, he was slowing down a bit, but then again, we all were. And at this point, I had to admit that it had become increasingly difficult to remember what life was like in a library that didn't have two feline employees.

Despite the visitors who showed up daily at the library for their photos and posters and pawtographs and the constant stream of articles and stories about the cats—which I dutifully clipped and tucked away in file folders in the archives— it still somehow didn't sink in how well-known the cats had gotten, and how much Baker & Taylor really valued their feline mascots.

The company had a lot to celebrate in the eight years since the first poster appeared. Bill Hartman told me that they'd given away 750,000 shopping bags, 250,000 posters, 200,000 calendars just between 1990 and 1992, as well as countless paperweights, T-shirts, watches, and other paraphernalia, all featuring the Scottish Folds that lived in our little library.

"It's hard to find a library anywhere in the U.S. that's not aware of the Baker & Taylor cats," he told me. "And when I go around and visit libraries, I often see one of the posters hanging on the wall or in the technical services department. Whenever we go to the library shows, we're constantly being asked what new shopping bag or posters we have."

The CEO and chairman of Baker & Taylor at the time, Gerald G. Garbacz, even chimed in. "Everyone at Baker & Taylor is proud to have Baker and Taylor as our symbols," he said. "We feel as if they are our personal pets."

Of course, we had to have a party to celebrate Baker's birthday, and it soon became clear that it was going to be a bigger celebration than we'd expected. Bill Hartman brought the human-sized Baker and Taylor costumes and initially the staff agreed to take turns wearing them. The day of the party, I was setting out paper plates and cups when I heard a muffled scream and saw one of the giant-sized cat heads—it looked like Taylor's—fly across the room.

"Get it off!" Constance screamed. "I'm sorry, I can't do it, it's too claustrophobic!"

"Okay, I'll do it," I said as I retrieved the head and gingerly slipped it on. I wasn't claustrophobic, but it did take some getting used to, as it was almost impossible to see because you had to look out the nose, which had two tiny openings. Plus, the head must have weighed ten pounds.

But it was Baker's big day, and I knew the kids would love seeing two human-sized versions of the cats walking around. So I put on the rest of Taylor's costume while Carolyn donned Baker's. I thought it would be kind of funny to have a photo of the costumed cats holding the real ones, so Dan rounded up the cats and placed them in our arms. Of course it was a complete disaster: they didn't recognize us and since they hated to be held anyway they struggled to get free. Plus, there was a camera involved, which in their eyes never ended well. Somehow somebody managed to take a few shots before both cats—the real ones—took off on a mad dash to the workroom. I felt bad for them, so I set out a dish of yogurt for Taylor and a slice of cantaloupe for Baker before the party started, and they momentarily appeared to forget their trauma.

We pushed the tables and chairs to the side of the meeting room to clear a space for a makeshift dance floor, and as soon as we opened the doors a crowd of patrons old and young rushed in. We handed out cat ears to all the guests and served cake and punch, though I didn't see Mr. Figini. A local guitarist strummed and sang Beatles songs as I ventured out onto the dance floor and vowed to stay in the cat suit for at least two songs before I bailed. But it turned out I was a popular dance partner—everyone wanted to dance with the cats—so I did my best to channel my inner Taylor while extending my arms like Frankenstein, since visibility was at a premium; though to be honest, the real Taylor would never be this sociable. At one point, I felt a small child latch on to my leg.

More than a couple of times that afternoon, I wondered how much Baker & Taylor were paying people to wear the costumes at the trade shows.

Later on, after everyone had gone home and the tables and chairs were back in their regular places, I figured that the fan club deserved a full report from the birthday boy himself . . . and Taylor too, since they had sent us a couple of books—*So Many Cats!* by Beatrice Schenk De Regniers and Ellen Weis Goldstrom for the children's library and *The Cat Who Went to Paris* by Peter Gethers for the adult section—as well as handmade cat masks made of construction paper.

Dear Class,

We had an exciting birthday. All the staff wore folded ears, one of the casinos donated two huge cakes, and we more or less slept through every-thing. YOUR artwork decorated our display case for the day and our pre-schoolers were doing some of the same projects.

We have sent each of you one of our birthday balloons—don't use them for water fights, please—and a bookmark. Have a really good school year.

Love,

Baker and Taylor

At this point, I considered Leslie to be a good friend since we had exchanged brief notes to accompany the letters from the kids and from the cats, and had even talked on the phone. If I didn't have time to slip in a personal note to Leslie, I'd incorporate some of my observations and complaints and things we could clearly commiserate on into the letter from the cats to the kids.

I felt like I could vent to her. She understood that we always operated at the whim of the library board as well as the county commissioners, and we all knew from past experience that none of our jobs were secure, and worse, that the cats could go at any minute as well.

If there's one thing I realized from living in the Carson Valley—as well as from the reason why I ended up here in the first place when my marriage ended—it's that life could turn on a dime at any moment.

Of course, realizing this didn't make it any easier, so it definitely helped to have a sympathetic ear from a fellow cat lover.

———◆◆◆———

While the vast majority of patrons loved the fact that Baker and Taylor lived at the library, I did realize that not everyone felt the same way.

In 1992, a patron filed a complaint with the state health department to demand that the cats be permanently removed from the library because of her severe allergies. She specifically cited the Americans with Disabilities Act, which was signed into federal law in 1990 and stated that businesses and public organizations—like libraries—could not discriminate against anyone who had a disability, whether it was physical or emotional.

And that included allergies.

From the first day that Baker arrived, we were hypervigilant about making sure that anyone who was allergic to cats—even slightly—could still visit the library if they called ahead, and we'd then put the cats in the workroom and close the door. We were also meticulous about picking up any clumps of fur we saw lying around and had the library thoroughly cleaned and vacuumed each week. So far, this arrangement had worked well for the patrons.

Employees, however, were a different story. After all, we couldn't keep Baker and Taylor locked up in the workroom all day and night. So the first question we always asked prospective employees was "Are you allergic to cats?" Most said no, and those with slight allergies took medication to alleviate their symptoms when they flared up.

We hired a woman named Maria Pearson and she proved to be an asset to the staff. But shortly after she started her job, I noticed that whenever she passed by the cats she stuck her hands in her pockets and basically kept her distance. One day,

I asked her about it and she sheepishly admitted that she was severely allergic to cats.

"I wanted the job so badly that I said I wasn't allergic," she said. "But I think Baker and Taylor know because they pretty much stay away from me."

I couldn't be mad at her. She loved books. And I knew all about wanting a job so badly that you'd do anything—even lie—to get it. Plus, she never had a problem.

But we still worried about the complaint. I was starting to hear about some other libraries that were having the same problem: while some ended up keeping their cats, others were forced to find new homes for their feline employees.

It was a tough issue: on the one hand, I wanted all patrons to be happy at the library, but at the same time, I didn't want our cat-loving patrons to worry that their days of spending a quiet afternoon in the library catching up on their reading while a cat snoozed alongside them were threatened. After all, we already had enough tension in town; we didn't need any more.

And I had gotten spoiled: I couldn't imagine working in a cat-free library, and I know that most of the other staff members felt the same way.

After a thorough investigation, the Douglas County District Attorney ruled in our favor. Our willingness to put the cats into the workroom and shut the door with some advance notice—along with the more-than-adequate air circulation in the building—was sufficient to prevent any allergy attacks, and showed that we were already following the letter of the law by accommodating patrons with mild and severe allergies.

The cats could stay.

But we all knew it was just a matter of time before another

complaint rolled in, and that there was always a chance that the next time the county would rule against us.

———◆◆◆———

As Baker and Taylor got older, they started to show their age. Both cats were taking a little longer to get from point A to point B, and sometimes they passed on point B entirely. Taylor in particular was having a hard time jumping from his afghan onto the floor, and then back up. So I started to help him up—or down, as the case may be—by pushing a low chair next to the desk so he could make the journey in stages if I wasn't around.

Baker was showing his age in a more unsavory manner. One day a little kid and his father were waiting in line at the circulation desk. The father had a look of disgust on his face. When it was their turn, the kid asked, "Do you have a cat in the library?"

I took a breath and launched into my usual spiel. "Yes, we have two cats named Baker and Taylor and they live in the library and—"

The father cut me off. "Well, do you know that one of your cats has taken a crap in the library?"

I asked for the approximate location and grabbed the roll of paper towels we had recently started to keep under the desk for such occasions.

"Over there." He waved with one hand while grabbing the kid's hand with the other before he headed for the exit.

For some reason, Baker had started to leave "presents" in the stacks, and he'd developed a clear preference for the history section, specifically the 970s according to the Dewey decimal system. Maybe he didn't care for the books about the Spanish

Inquisition because of how they treated cats, I don't know. But soon Dan was referring to them as Baker's bombing runs. "It's like the Royal Air Force over Schweinfurt," he joked.

Another time we overheard a little girl say, "Mommy, Mommy, there's Play-Doh on the floor!" Carolyn and I looked at each other. Again I grabbed the paper towels and thankfully I arrived before the little girl had a chance to play with it.

After that, we got in the habit of walking around before the doors opened to make sure Baker hadn't left us any more "gifts" in between the time that we let the cats out of the work-room and when we unlocked the front doors. I cleaned the litter box regularly, but from years of having cats, I knew that some older felines simply formed new habits that could be an-noying to others, and this was one of them.

So do humans for that matter, so I cut the cats some slack, as did most patrons and staff. We hoped we could recognize the signs and ease both cats into retirement when they appeared to be ready. After all, both cats had been around for more than a decade, and as things turned out, all three of us were thinking about our future retirement at the same time. As my own plan-ning for my nonworking life kicked into high gear—I set my tar-get date as 1997—we started to talk about the cats' successors.

Baker & Taylor—the company—was also thinking about it. After all, librarians all over the world had come to associate the cats with the company. It would be close to impossible for the company to find another symbol that created such goodwill—and sales figures—in their target market of librarians and booksellers. And so we all started to discuss who would care for the cats once I retired as well as the library's future feline residents.

Baker & Taylor offered to pay all expenses to acquire a new pair of Scottish Folds for the library when the time came. And while we appreciated their generous offer, none of us were a hundred percent comfortable with that idea.

First of all, any cat lover knows that cats everywhere can be ornery and difficult. And a library cat has to have a particular personality in order to deal with the different kinds of people who come in all day long: they should be friendly—at least some of the time—and not bite or scratch when stressed. I'd be the first to admit that we really lucked out when we brought Baker and Taylor on board, but another part of the equation was finding the right kind of person to care for them. In the beginning, I shared caretaking responsibilities for Baker and Taylor with Yvonne, and other staff members occasionally pitched in, but once Yvonne retired, the task of caring for the cats, buying food and litter, scooping the poop, and taking them to the vet all fell to me. In fact, the staff had long referred to the cats as "Jan's cats" and me as "the cats' mother," though a few also called me the cats' "publicity agent."

During this process, the library's board of directors was also mulling the question over; after all, they had the final say over whether a new pair of cats would live in the library after Baker and Taylor had retired or gone on to Kitty Heaven. The rest of us—including the Baker & Taylor company—really had no say in the matter.

⟐

In the meantime, the cats' fame continued to grow exponentially. I had to add another box to the archives as letters and drawings from the fan club poured in, along with cards and fan mail from librarians and laypeople alike. Although cat magazines and library trade journals ran stories about the cats on a regular basis, the posters that hung in libraries all over the country were far more effective at increasing the popularity of Baker and Taylor the cats as well as Baker & Taylor the company.

I was tickled when the cats were asked to supply a blurb for *Cats at Work,* a small hardcover gift book featuring color photos and brief profiles of other "feline employees," mostly in and around New York City. They ranged from hardworking cats in shoe repair shops and record stores to bars and delis. My favorites were the four cat employees at a clothing store who all wore shoplifting sensors attached to their collars to prevent them from walking out the front door.

Baker and Taylor's blurb was prominently displayed on the back cover of the book: "The diversity of working cats all over the world is celebrated through these stylish portraits. This book is a well-deserved and long-overdue tribute to our colleagues everywhere."

It seemed that almost overnight, books and cats had become immensely popular. Author Lilian Jackson Braun was writing a series of "The Cat Who" mysteries starring two Siamese cats named Koko and Yum Yum, while in 1992, author Carole Nelson Douglas decided to launch a new mystery series starring a black feline detective by the name of Midnight Louie. The first book, *Catnap*—later retitled *Cat in an Alphabet Soup*—was set at the annual American Booksellers Association convention, the same place where Baker & Taylor had a sizable booth each year and where they had introduced the human-sized Baker and Taylor costumes that we had found to be so challenging to wear at Baker's tenth-birthday party.

In Douglas's novel, Baker and Taylor themselves appear at the show, but are kidnapped from the booth, and Midnight Louie sets out with his human sidekick—a red-haired public relations expert named Temple Barr—to find the cats in Las Vegas, where the convention was held. I wasn't crazy about the plot; for one, I thought that it would give people unsavory ideas about abducting the real cats. But the book sold so well that Midnight Louie was soon starring in a new mystery book every year.

Shortly after *Catnap* was published, a filmmaker named Gary Roma contacted me about featuring Baker and Taylor in a documentary he was making about library cats to be called *Puss in Books*. He thought there was a sizable audience for the video due to the increasing awareness of library cats, from Baker and Taylor to an orange cat named Dewey who lived in a small-town library in Spencer, Iowa, and he promised to visit us in Minden at some time in the future so he could feature our cats in the documentary, too.

At this point, I was spending around an hour each day on tasks related to Baker and Taylor, from writing letters and sending posters to fans to speaking with reporters and journalists. I dealt with the extra work by coming in earlier and leaving a little later at night. I started to wonder if we could handle any more attention, the staff as well as the cats.

THE BAKER AND TAYLOR SONG

When Leslie Kramm sat down to compose "The Baker and Taylor Song" to celebrate Baker's birthday, she went about it in a matter-of-fact way: "I picked out bits and pieces from all of the letters that Jan had written back to us, and incorporated them into the song," she said. "The things that they eat and the things that they do are really true. The only thing I wrote that really isn't true is 'They're literate felines and that is a fact,' although my class at the time seemed to think so."

Here's the song in its entirety.

> *CHORUS: Baker and Taylor are library cats,*
> *They're literate felines and that is a fact.*
> *They live among volumes of books on the shelves,*
> *And love to read stories all by themselves!*
>
> *They're pedigree cats of the Scottish persuasion,*
> *But they don't wear kilts for any occasion.*
> *Their ears are folded like caps on their heads,*
> *So they always look ready to jump into bed.*
>
> *Gray and white Baker likes to lie in the sun,*
> *Or under desk lamps (but that's not as much fun),*
> *He forecasts bad storms just like weather men do,*
> *But by hiding in bags! (But a box would do, too!)*

Brown and white Taylor is a true food gourmet.
His goal is to move dinner up an hour each day.
When that doesn't work he knows just what to do,
He'll stare at your lunch and sit there and drool!

SEVENTEEN

———◦•◦———

In the spring of 1994, Baker was twelve years old and Taylor was eleven, respectively eighty-four and seventy-seven in people years, or so the theory goes. They had both gradually slowed down.

But then, so had I.

Fortunately, the county gave us the go-ahead to hire more staff. Us old-timers were still struggling with the new technology that seemed to show up at the library almost every week, promising to make our work easier and go faster. The newer, younger staff members were more comfortable with computers and could breeze through those thick-as-a-brick manuals on their lunch breaks.

So a palpable sense of relief grew among us veterans when we saw that the library was in good hands as one by one our retirement dates inched closer. The new staffers were also more skilled: most libraries now required high-level employees to have a graduate degree in library science, a far cry from when I got hired because I loved books and essentially handed in a résumé scrawled on a cocktail napkin.

I could see the writing on the wall: I still loved my job and the people I worked with, both patrons and staff. But I was getting tired. Nineteen ninety-four marked my sixteenth year at the library and I was closing in on sixty-five. I'd been working for almost fifty years, and it was time to pull the throttle back.

⸻

No one ever likes to think about mortality, and we didn't spend time ruminating over it with regard to Baker and Taylor. Then again, with so many fervent and experienced cat owners on the library staff, we were all too familiar with how short a feline's life span can be, which is probably why the subject rarely came up among us.

Of course, the cats had minor illnesses through the years, but I figured the breed came from strong, sturdy peasant stock and they basically just purred along day to day until the one fateful day when they didn't. In June of 1994, I noticed that Baker had become quieter than usual, and he started to hang out with the staff more—like Taylor—instead of sucking up to patrons at the circ desk. We kept a close watch on him because for a very outgoing cat, this seemed unusual, but we didn't think it was anything more than a passing late-spring cold since he was still chowing down on his normal amount of food.

But one day in late June, he was having trouble breathing so I made an appointment with Dr. Gorrindo. Baker struggled a little as I put him into the carrier, but a lot less than usual.

While Bob examined him, I made a mental list of the food I'd need to pick up at the market to trick him into swallowing the pills Bob would invariably prescribe: chicken, tuna, Fancy Feast. But when Bob lowered his stethoscope and looked away, my heart sank.

Baker's lungs had filled with fluid, and in a quiet voice Bob told me that there was nothing he could do.

Back when I first moved in with my parents in Genoa, I somehow became the person that the men around town could turn to when it came time to put their old ranch and hunting dogs out of their misery. They just couldn't bring themselves to do it. I'm not talking about taking the dog out behind the barn with a rifle, as was the custom on many farms and ranches; these men couldn't even bring the dog to the vet to get euthanized, as if they'd somehow be implicated in the dog's death.

They tried, oh, how they tried. They'd get halfway to the vet's office and have to turn around. But somewhere along the way, they came to know I would do it, don't ask me how. So back when I was living on the ranch and I heard my mother call for me when an old battered pickup had just pulled up in our dooryard, I knew what was coming next.

"I can't do it," the man would say by way of apology to me, his voice all quavery. Meanwhile, his most loyal friend in the world rested his mostly toothless drooling head on his lap as his tail thumped against the door.

I knew he'd never wash those pants again.

"Okay," I said. "I'll take him."

We gingerly placed the dog across the backseat of my car, and even though every touch must have shot through the animal with a sharp bolt of pain, not once did he bare his teeth or nip at us. As I drove, the dog would occasionally lift his head to stare at me in the rearview mirror.

How—and why—did I do it? I could never bear to see anyone—human or animal—suffer. Simple as that. But for well over a year, every time I ran into the man, his eyes would well up.

Of course, I had to put my own cats to sleep through the years, and it never got any easier. But this time it would be much worse.

After all, Baker wasn't just *my* cat; millions of people around the world loved him.

"Do you want some time?" Bob asked, his voice still hushed.

"Yes, please."

"Take all the time you need," he said as he gently shut the door behind him.

I listened to Baker's ragged breaths as I watched my fingers disappear up to the knuckle in his fur, which always made me feel better. But this time, it didn't work.

Baker's breathing suddenly relaxed, and I instantly perked up. Maybe he's better, I hoped against hope. But then I remembered that Bob had already administered a sedative to calm him.

I don't know how long I sat there, but finally I decided it was time. I willed myself to open the door, and nodded to Bob, who had been standing right outside the room the whole time.

I petted Baker and watched Bob prepare the syringe. "I'm really sorry," he said.

"Me, too," I said, my voice cracking.

———◦◦◦———

If you start having an epileptic seizure, don't expect me to get scared off. I'll wad up a piece of cloth and stick it in your mouth so you don't bite your tongue, and only then will I call for help. I never could understand people who have screaming fits and get all hysterical during an emergency. Really, what good does it do, for you or anybody else?

I've always been someone to call on in a crisis, that's just the way I am. Only after I take care of whatever unpleasant business has to be done do I go home and scream and gnash my teeth and throw the china against the wall.

After I left Bob's office, I knew there was no point in going home. Besides, there was work to do: I had to get the word out that we had lost one of our beloved employees. As I drove back to the library, I rehearsed how I was going to break the news. After all, no one—including me—thought I'd be coming back from the vet's office with an empty carrier and no Baker.

After I told everyone what had happened and the news spread around the library, first among the staff and then the patrons, soon there wasn't a dry eye anywhere in the building.

I had regular duty at the circulation desk that day, but I couldn't face the idea of telling people about Baker a hundred times or more. Fortunately, Dan and the others pinch-hit for me. Besides, if I was in the workroom, I wouldn't have to see patrons start crying as soon as they heard the news, which of course ended up backfiring because every couple of minutes I still heard people say "Oh no!" and "What happened?" the whole time I was sitting at my desk.

The next thing was to let the fan club know. I had to write as myself, not as Taylor or as Baker from kitty heaven, which wouldn't be fair.

It was close to the end of the school year, so I thought that Leslie would want to tell her class before they left for the summer.

Dear Class,

    I've just returned from the vet's office and have some sad news.

    A few days ago, Baker started to feel sick, so today I took him to his doctor. He discovered that Baker's lungs had filled up with fluid. There was no medicine or operation that would make him feel better, so together we made the decision to end his suffering and put him to sleep.

    He will be missed by his nephew Taylor who shared everything with his uncle Baker. He will be missed most of all by his library family, the staffers who shared bits of chicken and cantaloupe with him, and by volunteers and patrons who brought him treats and sent him postcards when they went on vacation. Baker didn't know he was famous, he just knew that he was happy in his home, with so many places to sleep and so many hands to pet him. We hope he has his own Baker & Taylor box wherever he is.

    Your friend, Jan

The rest of the afternoon flew by in a blur. I took parts of the letter I'd sent to the fan club and composed a notice that I sent to the local paper and the library magazines. Then I called Baker & Taylor to let them know that one of their beloved mascots had died.

When I had called and written everyone I thought should know that Baker had died, I packed up my things and headed home.

Only then did I collapse.

⋘•⋙

The next day, the "Oh no!"s and "What happened?"s continued at the circ desk at least once every five minutes as patrons
learned about Baker.

I braced myself for one patron in particular. The new issue
of *People* magazine arrived today, which meant Mr. Figini
would be in. I had no idea how he'd react to the news.

When he came, he ran through his "How are you today,
Jan? How is Mr. Doyle?" list as usual. Then he paused. "Is
Baker okay?"

I swallowed hard.

"Baker died, Mr. Figini," I managed to say. "I'm sorry."

He didn't frown or look sad. Instead, he just looked confused. "Baker died?"

I nodded.

"When?"

"Yesterday."

He turned away and walked into the reading room. He pulled
his *People* from the rack, sat down, and started reading.

Oh good, I thought. He's taking it well, a lot better than the
rest of us.

But fifteen minutes later, he was back at the circ desk. "Is
Baker okay?" he asked.

"No, Mr. Figini, he died."

Again a look of bewilderment crossed his face and he
walked away, this time heading toward the Biography section.
I tried to concentrate on checking in returned books, but it
was difficult to focus on anything.

So I decided to make a sign for the desk to announce Baker's
death. After all, Mr. Figini wasn't the only one asking where he
was. I essentially re-created the letter I had sent to the fan club.

As I propped it up on the counter, Mr. Figini returned. "Where's Baker?"

Someone else might have lost her temper at that point, but I understood perfectly. Like Mr. Figini, I wasn't a big fan of change, and when I'd had the rug pulled out from under me almost twenty-five years ago, it took me a long time to process the information, too.

"Baker died, Mr. Figini," I said. "So we all have to be very kind to Taylor."

"Because he misses Baker?"

"Yes, very much. We all miss Baker. But it's okay to miss Baker."

He went back out into the library, and we repeated the routine several more times that day. It was almost like he was thinking it over and coming back to verify the new information with me.

One of those times, I watched as Mr. Figini, instead of going to the reading room or the Biography section, walked all over the library looking under chairs that were pushed under tables, on shelves, behind rows of books, even in the children's section. After he made a couple of circuits around the library, he left without checking out any books.

When he returned the next day, he delivered his usual litany but he didn't ask about Baker.

"How's Taylor?" he asked.

I bit my lip. "He's still sad," I said. "And it's okay to be sad."

He pushed his books toward me. "Oh." He looked down and scrunched up his mouth a little. Then he headed over to the biographies.

I had to give him a lot of credit. Mr. Figini had had to

eliminate one of the questions from his routine, which couldn't have been easy for him. But once he did, he was fine, and it was as if Baker had never even existed, at least in the way he viewed the world, which was to blot out the pain and just get on with life.

Yet another thing that Mr. Figini and I had in common.

Somehow we muddled through. But at least once a day we were freshly reminded that Baker was gone when patrons and cat tourists who hadn't heard the news asked for him. If Facebook and Twitter had been around at the time, people would have known about Baker's death ten minutes after it happened. But in 1994, it could take several months until a magazine printed a notice, and even then many people wouldn't see it, which made things emotionally difficult for us on an ongoing basis.

It was especially hard to explain to the little kids who had spent time with Baker that he was in kitty heaven now. It often fell to me to console them, which oddly enough helped me feel better because I was regularly reminded of how much people loved him.

Planning Baker's memorial ceremony definitely helped. We scheduled it for Baker's birthday, October 6, and decided to dedicate a plaque and plant a hawthorn tree in his memory. Baker & Taylor donated money as did little kids who stood on their tiptoes at the circulation desk, dumping fistfuls of change and damp crumpled-up dollar bills into the jar for his memorial fund.

A steady stream of sympathy cards and gifts in the form of catnip mice for Taylor started to arrive almost immediately.

Librarians from around the country called to offer their con-dolences, and patrons donated books in memory of Baker.

A letter arrived from Martin Ellis, a library director in North Sydney, Australia, that I thought perfectly captured how people around the world viewed our two unassuming library cats.

"We feel we knew him," Ellis wrote. "A big poster of him and Taylor hangs in our workroom and his grave sensible little face has often been a source of joy for us all. On behalf of our admirers here, may I thank you for taking such obvious good care of him. I think he deserves a place next to Dr. Johnson's 'Hodge' as one of the great literary cats."

I couldn't have said it better.

EIGHTEEN

Of course, everyone was sad when Baker died. But what made things worse was to see how Taylor reacted when he finally realized that Baker had been away from the library for longer than usual.

Even though they weren't joined at the hip, the cats were very rarely separated throughout their lives. A few days after Baker's death, Taylor started to look for Baker. He'd probably figured Baker had been gone long enough; after all, the longest either one had spent at the vet was two nights. He made a couple of loops around the library, checking in all his usual haunts, but Baker wasn't there. Taylor came back into the workroom, made a noise like *hmph,* and jumped up onto his afghan.

Maybe he'll come back tomorrow.

But he didn't. After another couple of days, Taylor became really upset and roamed around the library for at least an hour, walking up and down the stacks, sniffing the shelves, craning his neck to look up at the tables, and calling out *mrow* every so often like he expected Baker to answer back.

But there was no response.

Then he'd try to open a few drawers; after all, Baker sometimes liked to hide in there. Next he jumped up onto the window ledge . . . maybe we were hiding Baker outside.

Still no Baker.

Then he'd *mrow* at us, as if he was saying, *Bring him back, bring him back.* I'd pat him on the head and feel horrible, but when it was clear that we were of no help, Taylor jumped onto the floor to resume his search. He'd march around again for a bit before finally flopping down on the floor, dejected and spent.

I knew how he felt. Even though I knew Baker was gone, out of habit I'd glance at his sunny morning window or at the top of the monitor at the circulation desk, assuming he'd be there. When he wasn't, it made me feel even worse for Taylor because of his daily fruitless searches. Whenever that happened, I'd find Taylor and pet him for a while. I gave him lots of extra attention. We all did.

This went on for a couple of months. Every day after I arrived at the library and opened the workroom door, Taylor would march out with great determination: *this* will be the day I find Baker. As the days passed, he got louder and louder and spent more time looking for Baker. Maybe he thought he wasn't looking hard enough.

Though we'd already announced that there would be no more cats at the library, everybody felt so sorry for Taylor that they thought surely we'd change our minds. Almost every day it seemed, someone offered us a replacement for Baker. Even Scottish Fold breeders wanted to give us a kitten at no charge, which wasn't a surprise. After all, we were partially responsible for building the popularity of the breed, given the millions of people who had seen the posters hanging in libraries and bookstores all over the country over the last decade.

Baker & Taylor also offered to supply us with another cat immediately, partly to keep Taylor company. To be sure, another feline companion would probably make us feel better and help ease Taylor's depression as well.

But ultimately, the decision was made for us: the library board had recently opted not to replace the cats. Though the last allergy complaint had been settled in our favor, we couldn't be sure that the same thing would happen when the next one surfaced. Besides, it was unclear if anyone at the library would be willing to commit and assume full responsibility for the care and feeding of another cat for the next fifteen years or more after I retired.

I glanced over at Taylor, and thought, "It's just you and me now, kid." It was true. Along with Constance, we were the only ones left from the original pack, since we'd been at the library the longest. Taylor and I were in the same boat. Our world had changed around us so quickly, between technology and the rapidly growing community, that it was becoming harder to keep up. We were becoming relics, well, perhaps me more than the cat. After all, as long as Taylor was still around, people would flock to the library. But otherwise why would they come to a library when they could look things up themselves anytime day or night on the Internet, which was faster and easier?

While the Web sites and online portals like America Online

and CompuServe that people could use from their home computers were pretty rudimentary in the mid-1990s, the developing online community was becoming a hot topic in the library world. How would it affect our jobs? If a patron could do all his own research, would we become obsolete? Would robots take over at the circ desk? Could patrons check out their own books? And for that matter, would there even *be* books?

Taylor and I became much closer in the wake of Baker's death. While Taylor mourned, he spent even more time than before in the workroom and at my desk. The only time he ventured out into the library was to wander the stacks and floor as he continued to search for his uncle.

But then a curious thing happened. After moping around for a couple of months, Taylor seemed to have had enough, and maybe he decided if he couldn't find Baker then he'd just channel him instead. So he started to hang out at the circ desk and roam the stacks, not to look for Baker—though he certainly still conducted his daily patrols—but to find patrons who had a free hand and nudge them into petting him while they were browsing for their next read. While he didn't become as social as Baker was—that cat would be hard to top—we noticed that it helped him feel better, which in turn helped us.

In September a new class of second graders automatically became members of the Baker and Taylor Fan Club, simply by virtue of getting placed in Leslie's class. Leslie had to introduce them to the cats by telling them that instead of Baker and Taylor, there was just Taylor. I didn't envy her.

I usually waited to receive the first package of the new school year from the new batch of students before I sent them a letter. But this time I wrote to them first since I thought it would make it a little easier for Leslie. I couldn't bring myself to write as Taylor quite yet without Baker, so I wrote as myself. In any case, it was comforting to know that a bunch of kids— and one very dedicated adult—missed Baker almost as much as we did, even though they had never even met him.

> *Dear Class,*
>
> *Baker was sick for only a short time. I got to say good-bye to him at the vet's. We all cried, but we knew that it was okay to cry. We won't forget Baker because he was special. Baker really loved everybody and almost everybody loved him.*
>
> *Taylor looked all over for Baker for a long time—in all the places he liked to sleep—and he meowed a lot. Taylor doesn't really like other cats (he's jealous), but he loved his uncle Baker and we think he was asking us to bring him back. Now Taylor is friendlier with people who come to the library. He spends a lot of time in a big chair so that people can pet him while they are waiting to check out their books. Be good and study well.*
>
> *Love,*
>
> *Jan and Taylor*

I also sent them a copy of the acknowledgment card we had mailed out to everyone who had sent us notes and sympathy cards. It was a blank note card that Baker & Taylor had had printed, which showed an illustration of the cats sitting side by side above the corporate logo. All of the staff members signed the card, and I wrote WE'RE SORRY, TOO under the logo. Then, I drew a pair of angel wings on Baker along with a halo on his head and added a few tears running down Taylor's face, enough to form a puddle at his feet.

Barely a week after I sent the letter, they wrote back. Leslie had the kids write sympathy cards, create bookmarks, and draw pictures of both cats. Every picture of Baker had him wearing a pair of angel wings and a halo.

They also sent a copy of the picture book *Old Cat* by Barbara Libby, the story of an elderly cat looking back on his life, to donate to the library. I read it at my desk while petting Taylor.

———◆◆◆———

Shortly before my alarm went off on the morning of September 12, 1994, an earthquake struck the Carson Valley. The Double Springs Flat earthquake hit 6.0 on the Richter scale. We couldn't get up to the Tahoe branch because the quake had caused several landslides on the Kingsbury Grade road, which was the main access route up to Tahoe.

With the last sizable quake that we felt back in 1984, the epicenter was in California, which is when the cats made the front page of the *San Francisco Chronicle* for waking up when the shelves moved. This time, the epicenter was about thirteen miles southeast of the library, which I thought was a little too close for comfort.

By now, I thought there might be a lull in the population growth, but people kept coming. I joked in a letter to Leslie that she should come visit "before we become completely urbanized," while adding "we have even resumed having earthquakes to try and scare them away." However, a few staffers pointed out that the increased seismic activity might actually have the opposite effect and make them feel more welcome, since most of the newcomers were still coming from California. But the main reason I actively encouraged Leslie to visit was so she could finally meet at least one of the cats. Even though Taylor had perked up considerably recently, he was still an old cat and quickly coming up on his twelfth birthday.

We held Baker's memorial service on October 6, 1994, on what would have been his thirteenth birthday. We planted a red crimson cloud hawthorn tree in front of the library along with a plaque. I had a fanciful notion of planting a white hawthorn tree for Taylor when the time came, so that their branches would meet in the middle and turn pink, symbolizing some wonderful thing or another.

We'd had Baker cremated and there was another deluge of tears at the vet's office when I picked up the ashes. As I drove back to the library, I smiled because I remembered how I used to open the window because Baker's yowls were so deafening whenever I brought him to the vet. In fact, he meowed so infrequently that I occasionally thought of bringing him outside in between vet visits just to make sure he hadn't gone mute. But once I walked through the door of the library and everyone saw what I was carrying in my hands, they all stopped what they were doing.

What should we do with the ashes? It didn't seem right to keep them at my house; after all, the library was the only home he'd ever known. But some people thought that displaying his ashes at the library was a bit macabre.

Then I got an idea.

The memorial plaque listed Baker's dates of birth and death, but you couldn't just set the metal plaque on the ground since someone could just walk off with it. From the years I spent at my parents' ranch, I knew you had to dig a hole, mix the cement, and set a post, rod, or rebar—or a plaque—in before it hardened. We occasionally ran out of dry concrete, so we used fillers like gravel or ashes from the burn pile.

Ashes. Hmmm . . .

Baker deserved to stay at the library.

I called the parks department and asked when they were planning to set the plaque.

"We're really backed up," the man on the phone told me.

Apparently the population growth was affecting their department, too.

"We can't get to it until next week."

Perfect. "I'll save you the trip."

"Really?" He sounded slightly worried.

"*Really,*" I assured him, as my finely honed talent for bluffing total strangers to give me a shot kicked into high gear. "I've done this a million times before."

And that is how Baker came to be buried at the library.

At the service, I gave a little speech and told the assembled crowd that it was important to keep in mind that while we all miss Baker, "he's not really gone whenever we remember him." We planted the tree and had cookies and cider, but no cantaloupe. It was out of season by then, and I was glad because I think that would have sent us all over the edge.

I invited Mr. Figini to Baker's memorial service, but I can't say I was surprised when he didn't show up, even though there were refreshments.

I think that would have been too much for him to process.

◆◆◆

Over the next few months, the fan club was back in full holiday mode, sending Christmas and Hanukkah cards and Valentine's letters, along with a copy of *The Valentine Cat*, a reprint of a 1959 children's book by Clyde R. Bulla and Leonard Weisgard about a cat with a heart-shaped white mark on his head.

Taylor still desperately missed Baker and continued to search the library a couple of times a week, hoping against hope that Baker would turn up, they'd bump heads in greeting, and head off to their separate corners like before.

I was happy to see that Taylor continued to interact with patrons a little more each day. He still wasn't up to Baker's caliber, but he came close.

He also channeled Baker's talent for mooching food.

In the next letter I wrote to the fan club, I told them that since we all still felt sorry for him, treats and lunch scraps had become part of his daily routine, and soon he started to gain weight.

> *Taylor is not really so much fat as "firmly packed." He does enjoy his treats and has managed to con each arriving staff member into believing that he hasn't been fed in at least a week. He is also heavily into lunch cruising, and the number of vegetarian lunch eaters is a cross he is unwilling to bear. He is a bad cat today because he licked all the cream cheese off my bagel, something he ordinarily does not do.*
>
> *He is getting fat and we have had to put him on a diet. Sometimes people eat a lot when they are sad.*

I was so worried that the kids had started off their year on such a sad note with the news of Baker's death that I was spending an awful lot of time writing to the fan club. In fact, it seemed that I had started to ignore letters from anyone who wasn't a second grader. So after years of sending personal replies to anyone who wrote, I finally put together a form letter.

> *Hello,*
>
> *Since I am almost 84 in people years (12) I don't do much rushing around the library anymore. Besides, I have some degree of arthritis. Sleeping is second only to begging for treats, which I do as each staff member comes to work. I am, however, a gentleman and never steal anyone's lunch.*

Which of course was a fib, but I figured no one had to know about the cream cheese incident.

> *I like catnip and turkey. I like having two litter boxes and I have my own mug for water. What more can a cat want?*
>
> *Best,*
>
> *Taylor*

It lacked the zing of my letters to the fan club, but I figured the recipients had nothing to compare it to so they wouldn't mind. I did, however, still stamp each one with the pawprint to personalize it.

<hr />

In June, Baker's memorial hawthorn tree bloomed, which was a big surprise since a grafted tree typically takes four or five years to bloom.

To me, it only underscored that Baker was a special cat indeed.

CAROLE NELSON DOUGLAS

Douglas is the author of over sixty novels in the mystery and fantasy genres. Her most popular mystery series revolves around Midnight Louie, a sleek black cat with plenty of swagger. She featured Baker and Taylor in Cat-nap, *her first Midnight Louie novel, which was set at the annual American convention for the book trade—then known as the American Booksellers Association—in Las Vegas. The book was published in 1992, and was later retitled* Cat in an Alphabet Soup, *and put Douglas—and Louie—on the map. In 2015,* Cat in a Zebra Zoot Suit—*the twenty-seventh book in the series—was published.*

Baker and Taylor were big in their time, they were just immense. If you went to any book convention, whether on the state or national level, everybody there was walking around with bags with the cats' pictures on them.

I always thought it was almost like a surreal movie where the director is showing you that everybody is regimented by wearing the exact same thing. In this case, everybody at the ABA was carrying a shopping bag with Baker and Taylor's picture on it.

Because I set *Catnap* at a bookseller's convention, I *had* to include Baker and Taylor.

When I first entered the world of book publishing, I had already been a journalist, editor, and newspaper reporter for a number of years. I was just stunned by how cumbersome and difficult the book industry was. I wrote *Catnap* because I wanted people to know that book publishing is kind of nuts, or at least it was a different kind of nuts back then. I had a couple of fantasy books published, but the world of publishing was so secretive that I couldn't even find out how many copies of my book had been printed.

Since I really wanted to show the reader how publishing worked, in the very first scene of *Catnap,* I murdered an editor. It was very fulfilling. Midnight Louie is the sidekick PI in the series, and though he's the one who actually finds the body of a dead editor on the convention floor, his main role in the story was to locate Baker and Taylor, who were kidnapped from the Baker & Taylor booth and held for ransom. In a mystery novel, you want as much going wrong as possible, and I like to have little mysteries—finding the cats—along with the big mystery—who killed the editor.

I gave Baker and Taylor Scottish accents in the book since they are, after all, Scottish Folds. Midnight Louie referred to them as having origami ears, and I picked up on what I knew about the cats themselves as well as the breed: they were rather placid and contented with their role in life since they spent most of the time hanging out around books while also being the center of attention. They had to be erudite and unflappable because people would be coming in and out of the library all day long, and of course they were very, very charming.

Their role in *Catnap* was just perfect, and they allowed Louie to display his ingenuity and his essential swagger.

When it comes right down to it, the cat and book connection is kind of amazing. People really adopt cats as sort of a symbol of everything that they think is positive in their lives, which is quiet, imagination, and a warm sense of connection with another being. It's basically an immediate mood enhancer if you sit down with a cat and a book.

Catnap proved to be extremely popular, and it went through twelve printings. That first book featuring Baker and Taylor cemented the fact that I was going to be writing Midnight Louie books for a long, long time.

NINETEEN

Despite the fact that Baker was gone, the fan mail and publicity continued. Gary Roma was wrapping up his work on *Puss in Books,* his documentary about library cats all over the country, and the last interview he filmed was with us. As we planned for his visit to Minden—he still insisted on making the trip despite Baker's death—I told him about the fan club and the song Leslie had written.

"I have to include that," he told me, and I put him in touch with her.

And then he came to Minden. He spent an entire day shooting video of the library, both inside and out, and interviewed me on camera along with some other staffers. I brought out a photo album and the archives and spent some time reminiscing about the cats. Of course, it was bittersweet when I told stories about Baker, and I was sorry he wouldn't be in the video because I'm sure that a shot of him lying on his back imploring somebody—*anybody*—to rub his belly certainly would have been a highlight of the documentary.

As Gary interviewed me, I remembered some stories about the cats that had faded into the background. Like the time a goose started to hang around the library taunting the cats and Baker and Taylor went absolutely bonkers. They liked to look out the glass doors that led onto a walled patio where birds and mice tended to congregate. When the goose showed up, he pecked at the door trying to get at the cats, who weren't sure what to make of a bird that was fifty times larger than the songbirds who usually hung around outside. As we watched the spectacle, I worried that the goose was going to peck right through the glass, when Taylor suddenly lifted up his front right leg just like a hunting dog on point. I don't think he was scared, just very, very interested. Actually, I think he would've made a great hunter and after that I occasionally referred to him as Pointer Cat.

When he was younger, Baker liked to do what Dan referred to as the "feline freestyle." He'd lie on his side or his belly, dig his claws into the carpet, and pull himself along in front of people. I don't know whether it was exercise for his claws or if he liked the feeling of his belly rubbing against the carpeting, but he'd cover about three to four feet before he stopped, turned in the other direction, and did it again. He was rather nonchalant about it, and unlike how he felt about walking his red bootlace, Baker didn't care if people watched him swim across the carpet.

Of course I didn't tell Gary about Baker's bombing runs toward the end of his life as I thought that would reflect poorly on library cats overall.

Perhaps the saddest part of the video shoot was when it came time for Gary to film Taylor, who had spent most of the day sleeping on my desk. Even though it had been almost seven years since the last photo shoot for Baker & Taylor, cameras of any kind still spooked him. But now it was time for his close-up.

Taylor wandered down the aisle toward Baker's favorite morning spot while Gary followed him, filming from behind. He moved more stiffly than usual, and though he didn't *mrow* for Baker, he paused at one point to look behind a row of books and turned his head from one side to the other as he walked.

I hadn't noticed it before, but now it was as clear as day:

Taylor never gave up looking for Baker.

I was glad that my own on-camera interview with Gary was done, or else I would have had to resort to drastic measures in order to fix my red, puffy eyes.

As Gary packed away his equipment at the end of the day, he mentioned that he had been to Spencer, Iowa, to visit an orange library cat named Dewey. I'd heard about him through the Library Cat Society, which was still going strong, and it sounded like patrons there loved him as much as ours loved Baker and Taylor.

Reminiscing made me feel a little better, but we were still reminded every day that Baker's death had left a big hole in our lives.

I set my retirement date for the end of October 1997.

In all the chaos of that last year before retirement, it some-times took me a while to respond to the fan club's cards and letters. One day, the students sent a note saying they were worried that Taylor didn't want to be their friend anymore. *Oh my God, what have I done?*

I wrote back immediately.

> *Dear Class,*
>
> *Please remember that I will always be your friend, and that Baker is watching over all of us to make sure we read lots of books. I still miss Uncle Baker and so do the people who come to the library. They are especially nice to me because I'm the only cat.*

I sifted through their letters and answered a few of their questions.

> *I don't eat mice, I get better food from the library people, and most mice are too scared of me to come in the library.*
>
> *I don't get very lonely because there are so many people in the library all the time.*
>
> *Since I read the paper every morning with one of the older people who come just for the newspapers, I follow a lot of sports, but I have to limit myself to ball chasing and the find-the-pencil-under-the-blanket game. My favorite teams are the Tigers (of Douglas County): football, baseball, basketball, soccer, volleyball, tennis, and swimming. They are all my cousins, I think.*
>
> *As for my job duties, I'm so old now that I just take things easy. My big thing now is depositing lots of hair on all of the chairs. Keeps the people busy with masking tape taking it off.*
>
> *Love from Taylor*

As I affixed the pawprint to the letter, it dawned on me that this was the first time I'd written as Taylor since Baker died.

Even though I started to pass some of my old responsibilities to other staff members, I vowed to hold on to the fan club writing duties as long as I possibly could. I always felt better after I wrote to the fan club.

⚬⚬⚬

Shortly after New Year's Day in 1997, a massive flood roared through the Carson Valley, bringing the entire region to a standstill. The library wasn't damaged, but the roads coming into town were blocked and nobody could get to work so we had no choice but to close the library. Just like last time, I was the only staff member who could get there since I lived so close, and I headed over each day to take care of Taylor. Since he had blossomed socially he had grown quite fond of his daily interactions with patrons, staff, and visitors, so when the library was closed and I didn't let him out to greet his public, he stomped around the workroom, clearly unhappy with me.

About a month later, a bomb threat closed all the county buildings, including the library. We evacuated the humans from the library, but not Taylor because we figured that whoever was making the threat was targeting the courthouse, the jail, or the sheriff's office; the library would probably be last on their list.

Between the earthquakes and the floods and the bomb threats, it was all in a day's work, I figured.

But I was tired. It was getting harder for me to do my job, which was partly due to age but maybe also because I had reached my saturation point: over the years, I had adjusted to a growing workload in fits and starts, by becoming more efficient and catching up on Sundays when the library was closed and I had to come in and take care of the cats anyway.

So I began to actively plan my retirement for the fall of 1997. I'd already decided that no matter what I did, I'd still come into the library every day to visit with Taylor. After all, the last thing I wanted was for him to think I had abandoned him, and for him to wander through the library *mrow*-ing for me, wondering if I was hiding in a drawer somewhere.

❖

My decision to retire was cemented for me on May 2, 1996, when my mother died. She'd been in poor health and had lived in a nursing home for several years. So while her death was somewhat expected, it still threw me for a loop. Her passing made me realize it was now or never.

After all, the apple didn't fall far from the tree. When I was growing up, my mother struggled with cooking, and cleaning was not one of her fortes, either. When I moved to my parents' ranch after my divorce, the same held true, so she took all shortcuts available to her. For instance, whenever she needed to clean out the vegetable bin in the refrigerator, she would get Pan the goat or Angel the horse—or both—bring them into the kitchen, and hold the door of the fridge open while they munched away on the old vegetables. I couldn't argue with that; after all, it was quicker and easier than doing it herself.

It seemed to me that I'd spent a lot of time recently reminiscing, about the cats and my mother, and the Carson Valley in the old days.

The day after the scattering of my mother's ashes, I immediately came down with a nasty cold, and it took a while to shake.

I took it as a sign that I was on the right track with my decision to leave the library.

◆◆◆

As he grew older, Taylor was shedding a lot more fur. Every few days I'd go through the library with a big roll of masking tape, and whenever I saw a clump, I'd scoop it up with the tape.

The fall of 1997 brought another school year and another batch of drawings, letters, and questions from the new members of the fan club. It felt a little bittersweet to write back, since I knew this was one of the last letters I'd be writing to them.

I looked over at Taylor, who was now spending most of his time these days asleep on his afghan by my desk. One month from now, I'd be retired. Constance had agreed to take care of Taylor.

I decided to take my time with the letter, and have some fun.

Dear Class,

Thank you so much for all your cards and the pictures. You all color much better than I do. I'm color-blind and can't draw. But I do have soft fur and a good purr.

Why do I eat so much? To tell the truth, I'm never sure if there is ever going to be another meal. You all know that El Niño is coming this winter. I don't know if that has anything to do with my dinner, but it is better to be safe than sorry and stock up for a long winter.

Right now I'm feeling strongly attracted to my baby bed—a Baker & Taylor book box that still has my teething marks on the edges. I also try to find all the sunniest spots in the library for my morning sunbaths now that it is getting chillier.

Well, time for my third afternoon nap. I don't know why people don't sleep more—can't think of anything that I'd rather do!

Love from Taylor

Little did I know that I would only be writing one more letter to the fan club. And that it would be Taylor's last.

❦

A month before I retired, Dr. Gorrindo had found a cancerous tumor during Taylor's annual checkup.

I asked if he thought Taylor was in pain.

"Not at the moment," he said. "Just keep an eye on him, and when you think it's time then bring him in."

My last month of work was consumed with paperwork, a few parties, and countless moments when I'd be in the middle of doing something and I'd suddenly realize that *this* is the last time I'll be collecting fines, or shelving books, or working the circ desk.

Though I always had a few books to add to the orders we sent in to Baker & Taylor, this time I handed in a list that was heavily weighted with the titles of mysteries I wanted to read and would actually have time for once I retired, as opposed to the catch-as-catch-can reading habits instilled by the time crunch of my job.

I spent most of my last day at work with Taylor, petting him and talking with him. The few times he jumped off the desk to head for the food bowl or litter box—or to get a small dose of people out in the library—he'd gingerly make his way down. Once he was on the floor, he'd shake out one leg, then another, before stiffly proceeding onward to his destination.

As I watched him, I could commiserate. I was moving the same way these days.

———◆◆◆———

On my first official day of retirement, I reveled in my new-found free time, but I missed spending my days with Taylor, which felt particularly acute because I knew that he wouldn't be around much longer. So I dutifully went to the library every day to visit with him, scoop the litter box, and gauge how he was feeling. After all, along with Missy Mac who lived at home with me, he was still my cat.

It felt a little weird whenever I was at the library: I had one foot in the retired world and one in the old world of the library. So I tried to just come in, check on Taylor, and then leave. During my tenure at the library, I rarely noticed the minute changes in the cats; after all, few people noticed those kinds of things on a daily basis. But now the differences were noticeable. Taylor was a little stiffer, took a little longer to rise from his bed, and he stared at the floor a few seconds before jumping off, hesitant to take the leap.

Over the next couple of months, I watched as he grew quieter and stopped mooching staff lunches. He was shrinking, both in his body and away from everything around him.

In the meantime, Constance had been carefully monitoring Taylor. She'd lived with cats her entire life, and as she later told me, "You kind of get to the point where you kind of know one day."

I already knew that, of course. But it never got any easier. Regardless of whether you had an animal for two days or two decades, it was still hard to say good-bye.

When Constance finally called, all she said was, "It's time."

"Okay," I said, and hung up the phone.

And so like many times before, I put my head down and focused on what had to be done. There'd be time to collapse later, although without the distraction of a job to help keep my mind off the fact that Taylor was no longer there, I worried about how I'd spend the days and weeks afterward.

I was especially concerned about the patrons and staff. After all, I knew how difficult it had been to return to the library after Baker died. But then at least there still had been one cat left.

This time, there'd be none. The flavor of the library would forever change. Before, staff and patrons could soothe themselves by petting Taylor and rubbing their faces against his fur; this time there'd be nothing.

And for probably the first time in my life, I was happy to be anywhere but the library.

But first I had to get Taylor.

It was just before Christmas.

I drove to the library and dug the carrier out of storage. Word had gotten out. As I walked down the hallway, some of the staffers said, "I'm sorry," while others looked away.

Taylor was curled up in his usual spot on his afghan at my old desk. I was about to pick him up, then changed my mind.

There was something I had to do first. I gestured at the computer.

Even though I was off the payroll, this would be the last

official duty I would perform as a representative of the library. I couldn't have possibly asked anybody else to do it.

I sat down and started to type.

Dear Baker and Taylor Fan Club,

I was so happy to receive your letters. We put them up in the children's room at the library where I live. Some of you asked me how old I am. I am fifteen. In cat years I am 105 years old!! That is pretty old for a cat. I am not feeling very well. I have cancer. Today has been a bad day and Jan is going to come get me and take me to the vet. He will put me to sleep so I won't hurt anymore.

I feel sad about dying because I will miss your letters. I always look forward to receiving your letters and the great cat books Ms. Kramm has sent to our library with all your names in them. We put your Christmas and Hanukkah decorations on our library Christmas tree. The angels you made look just like me! Now I will be a real angel in Cat Heaven.

I paused. It had been two months since I last sat in this chair. It felt so familiar, but at the same time it was worlds away. Too many endings and so few ideas as to what came next.

I would like Ms. Kramm to read you a story called Cat Heaven *by Cynthia Rylant. I am going to Cat Heaven and see Baker. I have missed him a lot.*

It is time for me to go. Thanks for being my friends. The Baker and Taylor Fan Club will always have a place in my heart.

Love, Taylor

I printed out the letter and started to fold it up when I remembered.

I didn't want to go rooting around in the desk, but the letter would be incomplete without it. I opened the drawer and pulled out the stamp and inkpad. I pressed the pawprint into the pad and tested it out on a piece of scrap paper. It was a little dry; I guess no one had used it since I had left.

I pressed down harder for a few more seconds and then, for the last time, I affixed Taylor's signature to the bottom of the letter. I don't know how long I kept the stamp there. After all, it was Taylor's last letter to the fan club.

Finally, I lifted it off the paper, afraid that it would be blotchy or that the ink had missed a spot.

It was perfect. I blew on the ink as it dried, and then I folded it up and put it into the envelope.

Now I was ready. I picked up Taylor as gently as I could and eased him into the carrier.

He went in without a fight.

⸺◆◆◆⸺

After I left Bob's office, I went back to the library and cleaned out the litter box, washed Taylor's dishes, and put his toys in a bag. No one said much of anything. For one, they didn't know what to say, so they kept out of my way. But I also knew they were quiet because they knew that it was the last time a cat would live at the Douglas County Library.

As I headed for the door, I saw the crayoned Baker and Taylor ornaments from the fan club hanging on the Christmas tree.

I swallowed hard. Dan and Carolyn stood at the circulation desk, their faces grim.

On my way out, I passed a woman I didn't recognize. She

could have been a new patron or a Cat Tourist. In either case, I knew what her first question would be.

"Where's Taylor?" or "Where's the famous library cat?"

For the second time that day, I was relieved that I wasn't sticking around the library.

Somehow I managed to drive the few blocks home without incident. Once the front door closed behind me, I collapsed on the sofa. Missy Mac jumped up next to me and I buried my face in her fur.

TWENTY

———◆•◆———

Taylor's death, like Baker's, was announced in an obituary that appeared in newspapers and magazines across the country. We buried his ashes next to Baker's, and set a plaque to mark the spot.

As before, the sympathy cards, donated books, and phone calls poured in. But instead of reading and then responding to each one, I heard about them secondhand from Constance and Carolyn.

Again, I was glad I was retired. I remembered what a struggle it had been to get any work done for the first few weeks after Baker died because every time a patron or Cat Tourist asked where he was, we were freshly reminded of our loss.

At least back then, we'd had Taylor to turn to. Now, three years later, there were no more feline employees. And I know that hit everyone hard.

"All good things must come to an end," Carolyn told Linda

Heller, a reporter from the *Record-Courier*. "Everyone here is upset, even more so than when Baker died, because it's all over. We had a good thing for fifteen years and are sad to see it come to an end. But even if we tried to replace them, they would never be Baker and Taylor."

Of course she was right. Still, after Taylor died, after the first few times that I ran into a patron at the supermarket, I learned to brace myself for the number one complaint: why aren't they replacing the cats? Some of the patrons were really upset that there would be no more cats at the library, and while I murmured my agreement, I knew if they got a couple of new cats—even Scottish Folds that looked identical to Baker and Taylor—patrons would still complain, simply because they weren't Baker and Taylor.

And if they *weren't* Scottish Folds, forget it; there would have been total mutiny.

The first time I bumped into Billie Rightmire after Taylor died, she told me she felt lost the first few times she went into the library. "It was like losing a friend," she said. "The library felt very vacant and a little bit cold with them gone."

I heard from Dan that Mr. Figini reacted to Taylor's death the same way he did when Baker died, though this time, like everyone else, he wanted to know when a new pair of cats was going to show up at the library.

"The cats had been a part of his routine, they were a big part of how he related to the world, and now both were gone," Dan told me. "He kept asking when we were going to get another cat for months afterward."

Carol, the children's librarian, had assumed letter-writing

and sympathy-card acknowledgment duties when I left, and the following February she showed me a letter she'd sent to the fan club.

"We miss Taylor very much," she wrote. "There is still cat hair all over the library and we may have to re-cover some of the chairs because the cat hair is embedded in the fibers. Just today a patron asked where Taylor was. People are still shocked that he is not here. Most of them expect us to get another cat but we have to tell them the library board voted not to replace our very special cats."

I didn't see the reply from the fan club, or from Leslie, for that matter.

In fact, I pretty much stayed away from the library. After all, I was retired, but more than that, it was depressing to visit a place that once had had so much energy coursing through the air, and all because of two cats with funny ears. Without the cats there, the place felt dead, the air was flat. It was hard for me to be there.

I still stopped by a couple of times a week—after all, I still needed my book fix—but honestly, there wasn't any reason for me to stay longer than it took to return my books, check out new ones, and exchange a few pleasantries. And I full well knew how busy everybody was.

For the staff, the change was more palpable: after all, a beloved longtime employee had died. It couldn't help but affect the library. Dan Doyle thought the overall feel of the library became more institutional practically overnight. "It wasn't your friendly neighborhood library on the corner as much anymore," he said. "It was still very personal, after all, it is still a small library. But the feeling was totally different."

While I'd like to think that my absence also affected the way the library changed, sorry, I'm not that delusional. But the cats had played a huge role in bringing—and keeping—the community together, and turning the library into far more than just a place to get books.

When I retired, I lasted about six weeks before I started to go out of my mind. I mean, how many times can you dust and vacuum and go out and work in a yard the size of a postage stamp?

I read of course, but ever since I was a little girl I had been accustomed to reading in stolen snatches of time because there was always something else I had to do: go to school, raise kids, work a full-time job, or correspond with a fan club. I'd spent almost every day of my life on the go for eighteen hours straight, and the adjustment to a relative life of leisure was difficult. It felt like going from 60 to 0 without a seat belt.

So when the entire day sprawled out in front of me with no schedule, I got antsy, and I couldn't focus on a book for more than a couple of hours at a time, which still left a whole lot of hours in the day. Besides, I needed to have some kind of contact with people each day.

So I took a part-time job at the county clerk's office, which suited me fine and still left plenty of time for reading and planning how to retire the right way.

After a year or two, I re-retired. The second time, it stuck.

In the spring of 1998, the last-ever letter arrived from the fan club. Leslie had sent it to Carol, who showed it to me the next time I visited the library.

"Sometimes it seems like just yesterday when my second graders wrote nine years ago," she wrote. "Those kids are now in high school. Talk about feeling old . . . It has been an invaluable experience for the nearly two hundred children who have been members of the Baker and Taylor Fan Club during the past nine years."

Personally, I couldn't believe how long she'd kept the club going. It's really incredible that she started everything just from that first poster, and neither the students—nor the teacher—ever got to meet Baker and Taylor. I always thought that was so astounding.

She also sent three picture books for the children's section: *Six Dinner Sid* by Inga Moore, *The Truth About Cats* by Alan Snow, and *Cat Boy!* by Primrose Lockwood and Clara Vulliamy. I always looked forward to seeing the books she sent—most of which I was unfamiliar with—because she had a knack for selecting books that really revealed the true nature of cats everywhere, and I'd miss that.

But it was official: the Baker and Taylor Fan Club was no more.

Gary Roma's documentary *Puss in Books: Adventures of the Library Cat* came out in 1998, and the premiere was held at the Museum of Fine Arts in Boston. At the reception afterward, he served bowls of cantaloupe and yogurt in honor of Baker and Taylor.

I watched the video when it came out, but when the camera

showed Taylor mournfully wandering through the stacks as he searched for Baker, I had to look away.

I wasn't alone. Jim Ulsamer, the former president of Baker & Taylor Books, later said he reacted the same way.

"When I watched *Puss in Books* with the scene where Taylor was roaming the stacks looking for Baker, I just bawled," he admitted. "I don't think I could watch it again, it was too sad."

As it turned out, we weren't the last interview that Gary had done for the documentary. He ended up traveling to Gahanna, Ohio, to film the current members of the fan club singing "The Baker and Taylor Song." They all wore T-shirts that said BAKER AND TAYLOR FAN CLUB, and interspersed with shots of the kids singing, Gary included cartoons of the cats acting out some of the verses in the songs. Best of all was the part where he superimposed the lyrics onto the screen, and in a nod to 1950s-era conductor Mitch Miller, who was always exhorting his audience to sing along by following the bouncing ball, Gary included a bouncing hair ball over each word to make it easier for viewers to sing along.

Even though their beloved mascots were no longer around, Baker & Taylor decided to keep using the cats in their ads and marketing campaigns.

"I don't remember it being an issue," said Ulsamer. "We wanted to keep Baker and Taylor alive with our promotional efforts."

The cats were still popular, so the company branched out with new ideas. In 2006, they launched a contest where kids could send in their drawings of Baker and Taylor; the winners would appear in the company's annual calendar.

At one point, the company considered getting another pair

of Scottish Folds and finding another library to take them, but as far as I know nothing came of that. So, instead Baker & Taylor scouted the country for a couple of cats that looked like our original felines. In 2009 they found two Scottish Folds named Mikey and Swayze and scheduled a couple of photo shoots with the cats, one when they were kittens and another when they were fully grown.

The Baker and Taylor costumes that we found so claustrophobic are still used several times a year at library trade shows, and like clockwork social media feeds fill up quickly with photos and selfies of librarians happily posing with the human-sized cats.

As for the Carson Valley, it's still growing, and people are still moving here, though it's slowed down a little, at least percentagewise; between 2000 and 2010, the population only increased by fourteen percent—or 5,738 people—compared with the boom years between 1970 and 2000 when the population of Douglas County went from just under 7,000 people to over 41,000, an increase of almost six hundred percent. With all of the new subdivisions, there are certain parts of the valley I don't recognize anymore. If you were to blindfold me, drive me to one of these new developments, then take it off and ask where I was, I honestly couldn't tell you.

But I'm cheered whenever signs of the old small town poke through, which happened recently when I answered my phone.

"Hello?"

"Hello! How are you?"

I didn't recognize the woman's voice on the other end. "Who are you calling?"

"My granddaughter up in Washoe Valley," she said, and told me the number. She was one digit off but it didn't matter. Soon we were going great guns about people we knew in common and how life was different in the Carson Valley in the Good Old Days.

We gabbed for close to an hour before we said good-bye. A couple of weeks later, the phone rang again.

"Hello?"

"Oh, did I miss the number again?"

"Yes, but that's okay," I said. "How have you been?"

And there went another hour.

Right before we hung up I said, "You know, we should meet someday," and she said, "Yes, that would be nice."

* * *

In the spring of 2000, my father died. Julia, Martin, and I drove to California to meet with the rest of the family.

Julia was dreading it. "I hadn't seen the cousins in I don't know how long," she told me. "All I could think of were all these stories about how these things go and I'm imagining fist-icuffs everywhere." It had been ages since I had seen the relatives as well so I had no idea what to expect, but I soothed her concerns the best I could.

When we got there, everybody wrote down what they wanted from my father's belongings, and my brother Tony and I went in the bedroom and decided who would get what so it was more or less even and nobody got upset. Afterward, we all went out and told stories, and it was just perfect. On the drive back home, Julia told me, "That was awesome. That's how it's supposed to be."

That's how it's supposed to be. Exactly. For me, libraries are *supposed* to have cats. I realized then that if I hadn't been retired from the library when Taylor died, I would have had to leave shortly after, because for me the cats and the library were inextricably entwined. One without the other just didn't feel right.

And I knew I wasn't alone.

—•◦•—

When Mr. Figini died in 2006, his niece Claudia Bertolone discovered that he still had a few library books checked out, so she gathered them up to return them to the library.

"That's the first time I heard everyone's stories about him," she said, adding that she'd had no idea how important the library and staff had been to him. This wasn't exactly a surprise since Mr. Figini was not one to talk about himself with anybody, even his family as it turned out. So when Claudia realized how much he loved the library and the cats, she got an idea.

She remembered how he used to water the peach trees back in California, so she offered to plant a peach tree at the library in her uncle's memory. No problem.

But then Claudia added something else: she wanted to bury her uncle's ashes underneath the tree. "That way, he'd always be at the library," she told me years later. "After all, that's where he spent his happiest moments."

When she was told that the powers that be frowned on her idea to bury human remains on public property, she started to think about a plan B.

But on the same day that the parks department was scheduled to dig the hole for the tree, someone from the library called to let her know that the hole would sit overnight, and the workers who planted the tree the next morning would have no idea what was in the hole.

Claudia got the message, and late that night she and her young daughter drove to the library and placed her uncle Joe's ashes into the hole.

At the tree-planting ceremony the next day, Bertolone and her family and the library staff stood around the tree and told stories about Mr. Figini. "We held hands and said a prayer, and then we all ate red licorice," she said. "Today whenever I go to the library, I always visit him. It makes me smile and breaks my heart each time because that library was his family."

It was yet another thing that Mr. Figini and the cats shared: the same final resting place at a place they considered home, and a family in the form of the patrons and staff at the library.

The cats were the great equalizers. No matter who walked through the door and what they needed, the cats didn't much care. They wanted a little attention—okay, in Baker's case, he wanted a *lot*—but they treated everyone the same way, except for the tail pullers and the occasional toddler who was in the middle of a tantrum.

Baker and Taylor were my coworkers, my ever-present feline staff, and the library was their home. Think about that for a moment: other than the eleven or so months each one spent at a breeder's home, the library was the only place they lived. They had to deal with a wide variety of strangers coming in and out all day—from small tots to ninety-year-olds with walkers—noisy computer equipment, and a daily dose of chaos and commotion. Most cats would never be comfortable with this arrangement—let alone the vast majority of humans—but over the years Baker and Taylor welcomed thousands of people into their home with grace and an abundance of charm.

———•••———

For better or worse, libraries will continue to change. Only now, more than thirty years after the first CD arrived at the library and we all stared at it, not sure whether it was a heavy-duty drink coaster or a small Frisbee, is the dust starting to settle.

Once upon a time, people looked to librarians—not Google—for help as well as answers to their questions about the community: Where do you go to see a movie? Which restaurant has the best New York strip? What kind of people live in this neighborhood?

And now they don't. As soon as anyone could look up anything online at any time, the writing was on the wall. However, these instantaneous results often lack the personal touch in addition to a few stray tidbits—and local gossip—that would never make it to the app.

This change has also affected the library community to some degree as well. With fewer requests for photocopies of original documents and interlibrary loans being made these days, there's far less interaction between separate libraries and their staffs. A few days of socializing and mingling at a library convention each year doesn't make up for the informal exchanges that come about when you have the only copy in the state of an 1885 newspaper article on Genoa pioneer Snowshoe Thompson, and everyone from third graders to adults researching Nevada history needs to take a look.

Don't get me wrong, acquiring information and knowledge

in any form is always a good idea, but when technology reduces the amount of contact that library professionals have with each other—and anyone else for that matter—well, in my eyes at least, the jury is still out.

In my opinion, this makes a compelling argument for why more libraries should take on a feline employee—or two. After all, no smartphone app is required to interact with—and benefit from—the warm fuzzy feeling that only comes from having both books and cats in close proximity to one another. And cats can definitely help increase social interaction at any library while providing a natural boost to patron visits. Anything librarians can do to draw attention to their library is a good thing, other than stripping at the circ desk.

But that's just me.

In the end, I'm pretty satisfied that I've had such a varied existence. I wish I had done twice as much, but doesn't everybody? What I'd really like to do is rewind all the way back to the beginning for a slightly modified do-over where I can selectively pick and choose: I would've done *this* differently but not *that*, and I definitely would have never done that other thing *at all*.

And why didn't I learn Farsi?

For that, I place the blame squarely on books.

After all, I've always been able to identify with something in just about every book I've ever read, or I've found something in a story where the author stated something in a particular way that really resonated with me.

Books were an escape. Actually, they still are. Even when you're learning something, it's still an escape. Books have long served as a drug for me; I mean, I *have* to have a book around. If I don't, I absolutely go through withdrawal.

It's almost like a compulsion, because in addition to learning something new on each page—indeed, sometimes in every sentence—I love to read because I never know what part of myself I'm going to see reflected back at me from the pages of a book. And if it's not exactly me, well then, it's someone I wish I *could* be. Some of it is wishful thinking, of course, but it's *all* thinking and you really can't complain about that.

I know that there are books I will never read. There are books in many languages. There are books that I just don't have enough of a life span to read. There are books that I don't really care to read. But I find that once I start, it's like a race. I just *have* to get through this book, whatever it takes.

But my favorite book is always the one I haven't read yet.

The flip side is that I've never been able to turn off my brain, which I think is sad. After all these years, it should go into dry dock for a few months for some repairs and to drain the bilge.

The only thing that I wouldn't change at all are the animals in my life, from Piggy the beer-drinking mutt to Pan the goat to—of course—Baker and Taylor, because along with books, animals have made me what I am today. I feel sad for kids who don't grow up with a dog, cat, or lizard. After all, if a child is deprived of interaction with other species, how is she ever going to get along with her own?

Baker and Taylor were great teachers, and in the end, I am grateful to my feline officemates for teaching me several vital life lessons.

The first thing they taught me is to be true to yourself. If it's in your nature to sleep twenty hours a day, as it was for Baker, then go for it and don't let anything get in your way. For Taylor, no one could stop him from sitting like a Buddha, and that was perfectly fine with him.

Next, be the best at what you do. If that happens to be sleeping, then take those paws, put them over your face, and just concentrate. For Taylor, holding staring contests with humans who clearly lacked the skill in comparison helped him to maintain his superior Buddha-like demeanor.

Lastly, never lose sight of your primary purpose in life. I'm not sure if Baker and Taylor had conscious goals, other than Baker's ceaseless quest to find the warmest place in the library and Taylor's desire to personally lick clean every cup of yogurt that crossed his path, but the fact that I never saw them waver in their determination helped me immeasurably in my own life.

Having a couple of cats live in the library could be time-consuming, but it was always worth it.

In the end, the library was the only home those cats knew, and they both were very happy cats. They loved the people and the staff and we loved them back.

In this life, I don't know what else you could ask for.

A LIBRARY CAT OF YOUR OWN

While most people love the idea of a cat who lives in their own library, they probably don't realize the amount of work involved both before the cat arrives and afterward. While I'd be the first to admit that we lucked out with Baker and Taylor, we did do our research to help us determine that the breed was probably going to work out well for us.

First of all, I would suggest that anyone who wants a cat living in their library—patron or staff member alike—to first meet with the library's board of directors for permission. If they grant it, then spend some time setting ground rules in terms of where the cat sleeps and eats, what happens if a patron objects, and who will cover the cat's expenses, among other issues.

One possibility: not every library cat has to have free run of their library. Some are restricted to workrooms, back rooms, and so on. In warmer climates, some are even full-time outdoor cats who have their own little cathouse outdoors where the staff feeds and cares for the cat, but the cat doesn't come inside.

Maybe you should start small, with a fish or gerbil, or even a bird, to test the waters. Then if that works out, a cat can be next. As for a library dog, well, while I'm not an animal psychologist, I think that unless a staff member brings the dog home every single night, a library dog would not be a happy dog.

Here are some more tips if you'd like to proceed:

- Research the breeds carefully, since some cats are more resilient and placid than others.
- Get a very placid cat.
- Don't bring in a kitten.
- If someone does deposit a kitten in the book drop, see if you can place it elsewhere.
- Don't bring in a feral cat.
- Also make sure that more than one person is responsible, to account for vacations and time off and weekends.

ACKNOWLEDGMENTS

First off, *grazie mille* to Scott Mendel of Mendel Media Group who helped shepherd this book with inordinate amounts of patience and grace, along with Elizabeth Dabbett.

Next, at Thomas Dunne Books / St. Martin's Press, thanks to Peter Joseph, Tom Dunne, Sally Richardson, and Melanie Fried. Thanks also to Sarah Melnyk, Staci Burt, Laura Clark, Kimberly Lew, and Joan Higgins for making this book shine.

Thanks also to Kristen Parsons at Baker & Taylor for helping to secure permissions to reprint the Baker & Taylor posters and photos in the book. And kudos to CarolLee Kidd of CLK Transcription for keeping on top of the hours upon hours of interviews.

Next up, grateful thanks to Constance Alexander, Claudia Bertolone-Smith, Charlene Cutler, Carole Nelson Douglas, Dan Doyle, Bob Gorrindo, Bill Hartman, Cindy Saddler Johnson, Carol Nageotte, Maria Pearson, Carolyn Rawles,

Billie Rightmire, Gary Roma, Leslie Kramm Twigg, Jim Ulsamer, and Linda Wilson for helping to flesh out the lives of the cats as well as life in the Carson Valley. Also thanks to the entire Douglas County Public Library staff throughout the years as well as all the librarians who have crossed my path during my tenure. And while I'm at it, a huge thanks to librarians everywhere.

Finally, thanks to my family: Julia, Martin, and H. H. "Tony" Haight.